Business
$mart

Mission: To Proclaim Transformation and Truth

Publisher: Transformed Publishing
Website: www.transformedpublishing.com
Email: transformedpublishing@gmail.com

Copyright © 2021 by Errol Beckford

All rights reserved solely by the author. No part of this book may be reproduced, stored in a retrieval system, or transmitted in any form or by any means without expressed written permission of the author.

Unless otherwise noted, Scripture is taken from the New King James Version ®. Copyright © 1982 by Thomas Nelson. Used by permission. All rights reserved.

Scripture quotations marked (NIV) are taken from the Holy Bible, New International Version®, NIV®. Copyright © 1973, 1978, 1984, 2011 by Biblica, Inc.™ Used by permission of Zondervan. All rights reserved worldwide www.zondervan.com. The "NIV" and "New International Version" are trademarks registered in the United States Patent and Trademark Office by Biblica, Inc.™

Scripture quotations marked (KJV) are taken from the King James Version (KJV) of the Holy Bible.

Scripture quotations marked (NLT) are taken from the Holy Bible, New Living Translation, copyright © 1996, 2004, 2015 by Tyndale House Foundation. Used by permission of Tyndale House Publishers, Inc., Carol Stream, Illinois 60188. All rights reserved.

ISBN: 978-1-953241-25-2
Printed in the U.S.A.

Business $mart

MAKE BUSINESS WORK FOR YOU
Why Some Small Businesses Make a Killing and Others Fail

Building Business in a Pandemic

ERROL BECKFORD

Dedication

- ❖ To my loving wife, who is cheering me on from heaven. Pastor Kim Beckford, you always encouraged me to become all that God created me to be.

- ❖ To all the small business owners of today, who have struggled, strived, and succeeded. And, to the business owners of tomorrow, who will see opportunities where others see failure.

Table of Contents

Opening Remarks — 1

Chapter 1: You Must Have a Business Plan — 5

Chapter 2: Intangibles of Building a Business — 13

Chapter 3: Choosing the Right Business Partner — 19

Chapter 4: Understanding the Market — 27

Chapter 5: Play by the Rules — 35

Chapter 6: Work Hard — 49

Chapter 7: The Power of Unrelenting Courage — 65

Chapter 8: The Winning Edge — 79

Chapter 9: Staying in Business — 85

Chapter 10: Surround Yourself with Human Inspiration — 91

Chapter 11: For Entrepreneurs Only — 105

About the Author — 113

Endnotes — 115

Opening Remarks

Business $mart Principle *Learn how to use your God-given instincts to achieve great success.*

While studying at New York University's School of Business, my professors told me as a business major that if I studied hard and learned all the principles of business, I would be able to build a successful business. Years later, having learned all the principles and rules of business, I became convinced that having a bachelor's or master's degree in business does not guarantee you will build a successful small business.

The best lesson anyone can learn from business school is an awareness of what it *cannot* teach you. Business school cannot teach you all the ins and outs of everyday business life, which are largely a self-learning process. A process that God directs. Which is why call it *The God Factor*.

I have witnessed a lot of small businesses start out great and within a year close their doors. I have seen every conceivable corporate style, culture, theory, and philosophy put to work, yet many still never make it. Through my experiences and observations, I crafted the advice that is part of this book's subtitle: *Why Some Small Businesses Make a Killing and Others Fail.*

Errol Beckford

Business Smart is for everyone desiring to start a church or building project; everyone running a business, or managing people and personalities; or those who are striving to get ahead to get things done.

Business Smart is all about the ability to make active, positive use of your God-given instincts, insights, and perceptions to get to where you want to go.

Starting a new business is no time for self-deception. Yet it is quite tempting to get caught up in your own strategy, business plan, or prospectus. After all, a lot of people are convinced they will never achieve total job satisfaction by working for someone else. Given the choice of becoming chairman of someone else's company or owner of their own small enterprise, many would opt for the latter. Starting a business has become the new *Great American Dream*.

If you only want to be in business for yourself because you are sick and tired of being told what to do, want more freedom, or feel unappreciated and undervalued—*forget it*. These are not valid reasons for starting a business, although they may be reasons for running away from your present job. If you only want to make a lot of money, that is probably not a great reason to start a business neither. Making a lot of money is a fine and worthwhile goal, but if it is your prime motivation it is not going to be enough to get you through the tough years.

Before starting my own business, I was cautious and apprehensive, but even more intimidated by the thought of wasting my time doing something I would not enjoy. I couldn't afford *not* to give a new business venture a try. I believe this great motivation is part of *The God Factor*. Most people (including myself) who successfully start a new business are fueled by a common feeling: *If I never try, then I will always regret it.* This feeling is what gives you the momentum to get out of the front door and to cut the corporate umbilical cord. It is also what makes it possible to keep going, even when everything else makes you feel like turning back.

Starting a business is a financial and professional commitment, but even more, it is an *emotional* one. I too experience rough times, when the negative outweighs the positive and any feelings of satisfaction are small compensation. During these trying times, it is the emotional commitment alone that *must* keep you going.

My main purpose for writing this book is to help small business owners become successful. Business demands innovation.

In *Business Smart,* you will learn:

- ❖ How to incorporate *The God Factor* into your business
- ❖ How to overcome *Fear of Failure*
- ❖ How to use *Business Smart* planning principles to achieve your goals

Now, let's open this tool kit together.

1

You Must Have a Business Plan

Business Smart Principle *If you are starting a business without a business plan, you are on the road to failure.*

Know Where You Are Going

Years ago, I learned the wisdom of knowing where you are headed. After all, if you don't know where you are going everywhere looks the same. No better story illustrates this truth than that of Julianne Koepcke. Julianne and her mother were flying over the Peruvian rainforest on Christmas Eve of 1971 when lightning struck their plane. Just seventeen when the accident occurred, Julianne later captivated the world with her description of surviving a two-mile fall into the jungle.

Initially, she had no idea of the tragedy about to befall her. Everyone was simply eager to get home and angry because they were running behind schedule. Ten minutes after entering a heavy, dark cloud, turbulence sent the plane jumping through the air. Parcels and luggage fell from the lockers. Gifts, flowers, and Christmas cakes flew around the cabin. When lightning flashed off the wings, Koepcke—who liked flying—felt fear. She grabbed for her mother's hands; neither could speak. The other passengers began to weep and scream.

After about ten minutes, Julianne saw a bright light to the left of the outer engine. Her mother said calmly, "That is the end; it's all over." Those were the last words she ever heard her mother utter.

Although the plane crashed, Koepcke miraculously survived. She was the only person on the ill-fated flight who made it out alive. By the tenth day of her frantic fight for survival, she was unable to stand properly, very wounded, and left to die. Nevertheless, she kept up the fight until rescuers found her. Even when it appeared all was lost, she refused to quit. She saw a vestige of hope, which allowed her to make it through the jungle and live to tell her heart-rending tale.[1]

Create the Plan

The above story illustrates qualities a business owner must possess to succeed in the world of business. Above anything else I will show you in this book, your business plan is the most important tool you will need to build your business. It functions as the lifeline of your investment.

If you are going to succeed in the world of business, you must have a concise business plan. It must be detailed and accurate, since its primary purpose is to give your business direction. It will also gain you respect in the financial community. Remember, your business plan is the best tool you will have to sell your business to the outside world and the most important part of starting up a successful small business.

The key to your business success starts with a plan. If you take the time to write a detailed plan, your business will succeed.

When writing your business plan, you must think your plans through and project their outcome over time. Outline your business from start to finish. Include details of everything from financial plans to management to marketing concepts. Remember potential investors want to see that you have the organizational skills necessary to start a business and see it through.

Business Smart Principle

"Good order is the foundation of all things."
- Edmund Burke[2]

Components of a Good Plan

1. **Format Your Plan:**
   ❖ Your plan must be small in scope, concise, and exact.

2. **Cover Sheet and Table of Contents:**
   ❖ The Cover Sheet should be the first page inside the booklet. It should have the name, address, and phone number of your business.
   ❖ The Table of Contents is where you will list major areas of the plan. Use subheadings as needed. Reference each item with a sequential page number.

3. **Three Focal Points:**
   There are three main areas you need to focus on when you are writing your business plan.
   ❖ Describe your company (include products and services).

- ❖ Explain how you intend to market your business.
- ❖ Summarize how you manage your finances.

Example of a Business Outline

Your outline should look like this:

1. Executive Summary
2. Background of Company
3. Target Market, Competition, Research, and Analysis
4. Business Objectives
5. Description of Products and Services
6. Marketing and Sales Structure
7. Operational Team
8. Financial Data
9. Appendix (supporting documents)

Let me define each of these areas:

1. Executive Summary

- ❖ This is the most important part of your business plan. Investors will see the Executive Summary before any other part of your plan. You must capture your potential investor's attention or else he or she will not want to read any further.
- ❖ Your Executive Summary should be a one-to-two-page snapshot of your business plan. Each paragraph should be only a few sentences long.

Key Elements to Include in Your Executive Summary:
- ❖ State the current position of your business. Basically, give a general overview of your company.
- ❖ Next, describe your goals and the strategies you will use to attain them.

❖ Include a description of your business; for example, what you will sell and how you will sell it. Lastly, include the projected time frame to accomplish your goals.

2. Background of Company
❖ Use this section to describe in detail your company history, products and/or services, and the type of business it is.
❖ Clarify the type of market you are in and highlight what makes your business different from competitors.
❖ Detail your location and any plans you have for future business expansion.
❖ List any accreditations or licenses that you hold.

Here are some questions to ask yourself as you develop this portion of your business plan:

- Is my business a sole proprietorship, a partnership, a corporation, or a franchise?
- Why will I succeed in this market?
- What is the ownership structure of my business?
- What type of financial performance do I expect?

3. Target Market, Competition, Research, and Analysis
❖ This section of your business plan is very important, so you should invest a lot of time in it. You must know what type of market you are entering. Here are some questions to guide you as you create this section of your business plan:

- What is the supply and demand for this item or service?
- Is this specific market growing or declining?

- How will you capitalize on this endeavor?
- Who are your customers? You must spend time researching your customers and identifying your target market. You must know who they are, including their ages, gender, and geographic location.
- Clearly identify your competition. What is your competitive edge?
- What is your pricing structure?

4. Business Objectives

❖ Be realistic when you are writing your business objectives. Investors do not want to see unrealistic expectations. Include your financial objectives as well as your operating and procedural plans.

5. Descriptions of Products and Services

❖ Products and services must fit together; if the product is a sail (supply), the demand is the wind. For the boat to work, you have to build a sail and find the wind to power it. For your company to succeed, you must build a product whose value proposition satisfies the need of the market and its potential customers. When designing your product, you should consider the following:

- Identify your target customer
- Understand the big customer need
- Know what you offer as a value proposition
- Design the product to fit the need of your target market

6. Marketing and Sales Structure
- Plan how you are going to market your business. What media platform you will use? Facebook, YouTube, Google, print, telemarketing, internet, or other means? Keep your target audience in mind when choosing your media platforms.
- When detailing your marketing structure, keep in mind your advertising budget, your growth factors, and geographical area.

7. Operational Team
- The Operational Team is made up of all the key players in the organization. Their roles must be clearly defined. Write a short paragraph about each key player and their position in the company, and include their prior achievements in other business-related endeavors.

8. Financial Data
- Include the financial data listed below in your business plan. Make sure your numbers are accurate. If they are not correct, it will ruin your credibility.

  - **Budget**: Include your assets and financing expenses. Some common expenses are accounting and legal fees, payroll, insurance, licensing, supplies, equipment, and advertising.

  - **Income Statement**: This should incorporate your future projected revenue, cost of sales, and operating expenses. This is called a "Profit and Loss Statement."

- **Balance Sheet**: Record your assets, liabilities, and equity.
- **Cash Flow**: List your projected cash flow from operating activities and how cash will be used for investing and financing activities.

9. **Appendix**
   ❖ Include all supporting documents at the back of your business plan, such as: market research, personal financial statements, licenses, and any loan appreciation.

2

Intangibles of Building a Business

Business Smart Principle

To everything there is a season, A time for every purpose under heaven.
- Ecclesiastes 3:1

In chapter 1, you learned the foundation of a successful business is to write a good business plan. Now that you have your business plan, let's start building the business.

Building a successful business is no easy task. It requires the application of proven strategies, which I call *Business Smart* principles. The information I am going to teach you in this book cannot be acquired in business school. This knowledge comes from lessons I have learned through my day-to-day experiences in running businesses and managing people.

The God Factor is the ability to learn and apply gut reactions to business. Building a business will require you to get the most out of others. This is what *Business Smart* really is: an applied people sense. Business in its simplest form always comes down to applied people sense and timing. With these two intangibles, you have the key to business success.

Timing

Many business ideas fail. They do not fail because they are bad ideas, nor because they are poorly executed, but because the *timing* is not right.

Business Smart Principle

"If bad timing is a disease for young businesses, then patience is the cure."
- Errol Beckford

Some years ago, my wife and I were involved in trying to establish a company called Alternative Behavioral Services. We encountered all sorts of unforeseen problems, including working with the wrong people and doing the right things the wrong way. These factors drove up costs, which prevented the company from moving forward. Our timing could not have been worse, and it cost us a lot of money to figure that out.

Still, I am convinced that Alternative Behavioral Services was the right idea and, given the right circumstances, this particular concept can work. When it does, I will be the one who will make it work.

A lot of new business owners are too quick to write off a good business idea. Simply put, their idea is good, but with bad timing it is not sustainable. When an investor says *no* to a project or an idea, it is not always because they do not like the project or the idea. They may have said *no* due to economic reasons, other internal factors you don't know about, or because the timing was not right for that particular investor.

Listen to Your Common Sense

The timing of building a business has any number of variables. It is not pragmatic. It is not a precept or a set of rules that can be followed. When determining the best time for you to build your business, be aware of perception sensory signals that are picked up by the brain, also known as *gut feelings*. Your gut feelings are a component of *The God Factor*. Consider your gut feelings to determine when to start or when not to start your business.

When you combine *The God Factor* with all the timing intangibles of marketing a business, along with how long an idea should germinate, when to present a business plan, and so on, you may conclude that timing is almost always a judgment call.

What this means is the objective factors of building a business are complex. Each factor, such as the products or services you are going to sell, the people whom you are selling to, and the location where you will establish the business will all give off their own unique sensory signals. These sensory signals are there for you to pick up on when making decisions regarding the timing of your business.

Listen to the Market

As the business owner, you control the time frame to start the business. Take cues from the market. Obviously, this places a premium on listening rather than talking. Really hear what the market is telling you, instead of paying it "ear service."

You can pick up a lot of timing clues just by asking the right questions. Remember, many companies fail their first year in business because of bad timing. Pay attention to timing before starting your business.

Instant Gratification

The urge for instant gratification pulls on us all. Everything about the corporate environment seems to increase this urge. Instant gratification is denoted by the pressure to grow *now* and make a profit or go on to the next thing.

We must remember we can't make people do what we want them to do. People and events move at their own pace and never go according to our timetable. One of the surest signs of business maturity is the ability to postpone instant gratification.

As someone who has built successful companies, I can think of no aspect of timing that is more important than patience. Lack of patience alone is enough for you to fail in business.

Persistence

Building a business requires persistence. When I was selling insurance, I knocked on a lot of doors. Many of them did not open. Through persistence and continually knocking on more doors, I eventually located ones that opened. By going back again and again, I achieved the desired results.

Sales and service businesses alike must have the *Business Smart* attributes of patience and persistence. Without patience to wait and persistence to go back again and again, any other insight into building your business is not worth much. Persistence is certainly right up there among the basic business commandments of *knowing your product* and *believing in your product.*

Business
Smart
Principle

"In the midst of chaos, look for opportunity."
- Errol Beckford

Take Advantage of Business Opportunity

Business ideas will drop into your lap. You do not have to be a fortune teller to spot them, nonetheless, you have to be sensitively attuned to their significance and have the insight necessary to tailor them to your advantage.

Take Advantage of Bad Business Timing of Others

The bad or unfortunate timing of others can create all sorts of business opportunities for you to start your business. You often see this in an election year. Each candidate will be very cautious as to when to throw their hat into the ring. They are waiting for others to make a political blunder so they can then ride in as the white knight.

Just as you should build your business in good times, you can also build your business when your prospective competition is hesitant.

Always Remember to Weigh the Present Against the Future

Famed entrepreneur and Remington Products spokesman Victor Kiam once said: "Entrepreneurs are simply those who understand that there is little difference between obstacle and opportunity and are able to turn both to their advantage."[1]

During times of a highly publicized crisis, people tend to save their money more cautiously, only paying high priority bills and purchasing essential items. This generally spells disaster for small businesses since it results in lower sales and income. Smart business owners know they need to spend money on sales and marketing promotions in the midst of a crisis, even if they have to borrow the money. When the sales start coming in, bills can be paid, and the borrowed money returned to the lender.

If a business only focuses on conserving cash by cutting back spending, paying off debt, and trying to save money, it will cause the economy to slow down even worse. Businesses and individuals following this course of action may not recover when the rest of the economy does. They will be far behind the businesses who implemented the *Business Smart* principles outlined in this book. Spend money wisely to move forward during an economic downturn.

During the 2020 world-wide pandemic, when many businesses closed their doors, I used the principles in this book to open a Latino restaurant in the city of Cocoa, Florida, even when others were closing their doors. In August of 2021, the restaurant celebrated its one-year anniversary amid great success. Don't let a pandemic or economic downturn destroy your business and your dreams in the process.

3

Choosing the Right Business Partner

Business Smart Principle *Choosing the right business partner requires insight and gut instinct.*

I can't imagine anyone being effective in business without having some insight into people. Navigating the intricacies of business successfully is such a subtle matter and involves creating a slight edge here and an imperceptible edge there. Every aspect of the process comes back to people: managing people, selling to people, working with people, and simply persuading people to do what you want them to do. Without insight, there is no discernment.

Insight allows you to see beyond the present. Suppose you had a way to know everything that was going to happen in business over the course of the next five years. That information would not only make you wise; it would also make you successful and wealthy. Henceforth, it is your insight into people that gives you the ability to anticipate the future.

A person's true nature cannot change with situations. Their true self is totally consistent. The better you know a person, the more you can get beneath their facade, and the more accurately you can predict how they are likely to react or respond in almost any business situation. This knowledge will be invaluable.

Insight demands opening up your senses by talking less and listening more. I believe you can learn almost everything you need to know simply by watching and listening. Keep your eyes peeled, your ears open, and your mouth closed.

Listen to People Before You Make Your Decision

The ability to listen and really *hear* what an individual is saying has far greater business implications than simply gaining insight into people in general. When selling a product or service, there is probably no greater asset than learning to be a good listener.

If you are going to learn to understand people, you have to be willing to learn to listen and observe them. When I am going to make an important business decision, I do not do it over the phone, by email, or via text. I will only do it face to face. I want to make my decision based on what I observe even more than what I hear. After all, the impression you get from meeting someone in person is quite different than the one formed when speaking over the phone, by email, or by text.

Observation

Observation is an essential key when choosing a good business partner. People are constantly revealing themselves in ways that will go unnoticed, unless you intentionally seek to gather otherwise ignored insights through observation. Pay attention to the statements people make about themselves and the signals they give off, both consciously and unconsciously.

Unconscious signals, commonly called body language, are certainly important, but they are only half of the story. Most visual statements are actually quite conscious and intentional, such as the way someone dresses, the way they carry themselves, and all the other exterior ways people go about trying to create a particular impression. Nonetheless, these signals are only as useful as your ability to pick up on them.

When I meet someone face to face, I primarily try to establish a comfort zone. So to speak, the comfort zone is the set of established boundaries I discern based on what I see and hear. This enables me to best deal with that particular person.

A word of caution: careful observation of a person does not mean jumping too quickly to conclusions, overreacting to your interpretation of their behavior, or reading deeper meaning into things where none exists.

It would be as foolish as it is misleading to generalize about a person based on their body movements or lack of, or to jump to hasty conclusions. Useful observations must be considered within the larger context of the situation and combined with what else you are hearing and seeing.

Eye Contact

Of course, the most fertile, consistent, revealing arena for observation is the eye. The eye will tell you, more than anything else, what someone is really thinking—even when all the other signs are pointing elsewhere. Remember that people communicate with their eyes in business situations when they cannot use words. The next time you meet with investors or potential business partners, purposefully observe their eye contact. It will help you to know if they are taking an interest in what you are saying or if you are boring them.

The Best Business Partner

When I started out building my business, I had an awesome partner: my wife. That is hard to beat. We had a great relationship. Our first business was a hoagie shop. She was a woman of detail, and always paying attention to the fine points of a situation.

Negotiation is one of my strengths. I learned negotiation strategies from observing my wife. She implemented three critical factors into her negotiations: pay attention to detail, actively listen, and keenly observe. Through her demonstration of strength in these areas and her ability to get results, I was motivated to do the same. Through her, I learned that business requires toughness as well as insight. My wife was such a hard worker that she could immediately sense if someone else was not. She taught me how to spot *time-wasters*.

Over the years, I have also learned to trust my gut instinct. You can develop this area, but it is predominantly an inherent talent. For example, there are times I don't feel right about a person, while other times I know right away that I want to do business with a particular person.

As an entrepreneur, you will have employees. I believe every person you hire is a gamble, no matter what their credentials. You can hire a person from one of the best schools and later find out they are a not-so-great employee. In contrast, you can hire a person without credentials, and discover they are terrific. And yes, there are still people who are who they say they are and do what they say they are going to do. It is important to give people a chance to prove themselves. I have been pleasantly and unpleasantly surprised over the years.

With partners it is a bit different. You cannot count on much of a trial-and-error phase to assess a person's qualifications. Here is where *The God Factor*—your gut instinct—comes into play. As I said before, it is difficult to explain how this dynamic works. It's an unspoken intuition that you must pay attention to. Partnerships must have loyalty and integrity at their core. Ask yourself if these two attributes are apparent.

If a potential partner has to talk themselves up too much, that is usually an indicator something is not quite right. Overly compensating verbally often reflects a lack of confidence. Confidence must stem from evidence of their ability to get results and not just talk. Remember you are choosing a partner, not an apprentice.

Negotiation

Partnerships require negotiation. It should be a win-win setup; otherwise, it is not a partnership. My main criteria for a partner is they must be an all-around good person. I do not need to be connected with any other type of individual.

As entrepreneurs, we rely on people to get things done. We had the original idea, but moving the idea forward can involve hundreds of people. Every person becomes integral to our overall success.

Doing It Alone

Over the years, I have had several conversations with small business owners about partnerships and how difficult they can be. Most of them were in the middle of partnership woes.

I prefer doing business by myself rather than having partners. Sometimes having partners can be too complicated. Unforeseen circumstances or differences of opinion can eventually sour the relationship, leading to the need to restructure the business or the worst-case scenario: its collapse.

My preference is to build business relationships without the unintended weight of the baggage a full partnership eventually accumulates. Partnerships are like marriage. They can be wonderful or terrible. As often as you are able, stick to doing business with people you like and trust. Then you can move on from there to build a successful business.

I do not have business partners because I work very hard and I work quick. I am not easy to work with because I demand a lot from myself. Most of the time I work by gut instinct. I am a risk taker.

You can have a successful business without partners if you are capable of structuring deals and bringing in the right talent for specific projects or developments. For example, if I am building a new building, I will bring in architect, who will in turn will bring in his team. I then find the right contractors, landscapers, and so forth. The process is complex, but worthwhile because the entire development is yours and in your control.

> **Business $mart Principle**
>
> *You cannot do a good business with a bad partner.*

Doing Business with a Partner

Partners are crucial. If you are looking to do business with a partner, he or she must be trustworthy. The person should possess all the skills and talents necessary to be your partner. Look for people who have the same values as you. Partnerships will not work otherwise. It is next to impossible to build a business among partners who do not share the same values.

Remember, not everyone is cut out for partnerships. If you question whether or not you can build a good partnership, it is time to look in the mirror and ask yourself why that is.

These words could be the most important words in life, not just in business. These are more than words of wisdom. These are guiding words—words to live one's life by.

Wherever you find a struggling business, a bad marriage, or an investment gone sour, you will find a failed partnership. This does not mean the people are bad, although they could be. It just means they had a bad partnership; they attached themselves to the wrong person for the task at hand.

The world is filled with a lot of good people, but that alone does not make them good potential partners for you in every endeavor. By comparison, within the institution of marriage, the world is filled with good people who are married to the wrong person.

If you attach yourself to a truly bad person, meaning a person with low legal, ethical, or moral values, no matter how good you might be, the business or marriage will go bad. If you have a bad partner, whatever you touch will turn bad. On the contrary, if you have a great partner, everything you touch turns to gold.

4

Understanding the Market

Before I get into the details of a marketing plan, let us clarify the meaning of the terms marketing, advertising, and marketability.

In basic terms, *marketing* is the process of identifying customer needs and determining how to best meet those needs. In contrast, *advertising* is the exercise of promoting a company and its products or services through paid channels. In other words, *advertising* is a component of *marketing*.

On the other hand, *marketability* is "the ability of a commodity to be sold or marketed." For example, a beautiful lawn will increase the marketability of a property.

Marketability

One of the most subtle forms of marketability is to build a perception into the product itself. Do everything possible to make your product buyable and the company trustworthy.

Marketability cannot be absolutely determined from market studies, market tests, or focus groups. Marketability must also be understood or worked out by instinct. It involves looking beyond one's own reasoning and perceiving the underlying motivation. This explains *why* someone really cares or does not care about your product or company. Marketability is a distinct form of marketing. There is a way to do it, before the fact, and if it is done correctly, it does not cost anything.

Marketability is the more active form of selling. Selling, by necessity, is product-oriented. Selling focuses on a product's features, functions, advantages, and so forth. Understanding your product's marketability brings the buyer into the picture. Is the product being sold directly to a customer or to a middleman?

My goal in this chapter is to connect the product to people. The route begins with the product and all the selling verities that affect it. The route ends with positioning. What you say or show about a product can practically sell it for you.

Business $mart
Principle

Know your product.
Believe in your product.
Sell your product like there is no tomorrow.

The Golden Rule

These are essential fundamental truths to build a *Business Smart* company. If you do not believe in the product you are selling nor know the product, people will resent your efforts to sell it. If you do not believe in it, no amount of personality or techniques will cover up that fact. If you cannot sell with enthusiasm, the lack of it will be infectious.

My most recent business venture has been helping develop a Latino restaurant. I once observed one of the servers trying to help a customer with the menu. Because she did not know the menu, she could not answer the customer's questions.

The customer was not satisfied with her inability to help, so they left.

Nothing turns off a potential customer quicker than a salesperson's lack of familiarity with the product. Have you ever walked into a department store and asked the sales personnel how a particular gadget or appliance worked, then stood by while they fiddled with the knobs and wondered out loud, "Why don't they make things simply anymore?" Even if they finally get it to work, by that time your interest has diminished and you are not likely to make the purchase.

All business owners building their companies using *Business Smart* principles must ensure they and their employees know the products they are selling to the degree that they are able to teach others about them. Knowing the product also means understanding the *idea* behind its purpose, how the product is perceived, and the relationship between the product and someone who wants to buy it.

Here are some guiding questions to ensure a working knowledge about a product:

- How will this product help the customer?
- What problem is this product solving?
- What are the promises of this product?

Understanding these intangible features is as important as knowing a product's mechanical features. Yet, because they are intangible and may even vary from customer to customer, they are more prone to being misinterpreted and misunderstood.

Knowing your product also means understanding the image it is projecting. All products project an image of some sort.

It may be a positive one, which you want to promote, or a negative one, which you need to overcome.

Anticipate All the Reasons Why Someone Might Not Buy From You

Part of knowing your product is knowing all the reasons why someone might not want to buy it. Anticipate the reasons. State them clearly in your mind. You must become the judge of your product before anyone else.

Remember, everyone's baby is beautiful, so do not deceive yourself by thinking your product is the best before you do a critical analysis of it.

Ask yourself these questions:

- How does my product compare to similar products?
- What is my *Business Smart* competitive edge?

For example: I am writing this book, *Business Smart*, in comparison to what? In order to answer this question, I had to research comparable books on the subject of building a successful business. I then determined that the competitive edge for *Business Smart*—which I expounded on in the Opening Remarks—is the application of *The God Factor*.

When I was putting together the menu for the Latino restaurant, the first thing I did was compare the menu to other Latino restaurants. With that insight, I was able to gain the competitive edge in that sector.

Let Go of Bad Ideas

Here is an excerpt from *What They DON'T Teach You at Harvard Business School*, written by entrepreneur and sports marketing guru Mark H. McCormack:

A dog food company was holding its annual sales convention. During the course of the convention the president of the company listened patiently as his advertising director presented a hot new campaign.

His marketing director introduced a point-of-sale scheme that would "revolutionize the best damn sale force in the business."

Finally, it came time for the president to take the podium and make his closing remarks. "Over the past few days," he began, "we've heard from all our decision heads and of their wonderful plans for the coming year. Now as we draw to a close, I have only one question. If we have the best advertising, the best marketing, the best sales force, how come we sell less dog food than anyone in the business?"

Absolute silence filled the convention hall. Finally, after what seemed like forever, a small voice answered from the back of the room: "Because the dogs hate it."[1]

Sometimes a plan, idea, product, or concept is just plain bad. No matter how much you beat it, no matter how you restate it, it simply will not work. The simple solution is to walk away. Cut your losses and run.

Yet, a lot of people try just the opposite. The more the evidence mounts that an idea may not be salable, a concept may not be workable, or a product may not be desirable, the more misguided determination, wasted time, and unprofitable spending that goes on in a vain effort to sustain a bad idea. Naively, I *was* one of those people.

Jesus demonstrates the importance of letting go of bad ideas:

> He also spoke this parable: "A certain man had a fig tree planted in his vineyard, and he came seeking fruit on it and found none. Then he said to the keeper of his vineyard, 'Look, for three years I have come seeking fruit on this fig tree and find none. Cut it down; why does it use up the ground?' But he answered and said to him, 'Sir, let it alone this year also, until I dig around it and fertilize *it*. And if it bears fruit, well. But if not, after that you can cut it down.'"
>
> - Luke 13:6–10

Key Components of the 80/20 Rule

I have spent a lot of time talking about knowing your product, believing in your product, and selling your product like there is no tomorrow. It is obvious how I feel about that.

> **Business Smart Principle**
> *80/20 Rule:*
> *80% of your business is done with 20% of your customers*

Most companies follow the 80/20 rule when directing their sales efforts. It makes sense to focus four-fifths of your time and effort getting to know the one-fifth of your customers who are the most important to you. A lack of understanding and application of the 80/20 rule has caused some businesses to fail. They burn up too much time focusing on the less profitable 80 percent, rather than spending the time to know the 20 percent that are making their business grow. Focus on the interests and tastes of your top 20 percent. Take the time to figure out what you can do to keep them there.

Positioning

In business, the word *position* has been known to express multiple meanings:

- ❖ A company *positions* itself for the future
- ❖ A product is *positioned* in the marketplace
- ❖ Individuals *position* themselves for advancement

With so many business meanings for the word, *position*, it can become meaningless. I am going to define it very narrowly, as it relates to your product or service.

> **Positioning:** a matter of determining what someone is really buying when they buy your product or service. The ability to communicate those impressions and motivation to buyers.

Foremost, getting into *position* catapults your *Business Smart* endeavor by converting human emotions into the characteristics of your product or service.

Be a Winner

The fastest way to become a winner is by sticking with a winner. The fastest way to become a loser is by sticking with a loser. To pick a winner requires intelligence, savviness, and forethought.

A *Business Smart* company must figure out where it fits in the marketplace and where its products or services fit. That *fit* becomes the target you must keep in sight. Put forth all your focus to meticulously hit the target. Streamlining for productivity is the *secret sauce* of marketing.

Marketing Plan and Advertising

Many small businesses fail to attract customers to their business. They falsely believe that just by simply advertising their business on a paid channel, customers will flock to their business, without them having to do the work of creating a marketing plan.

When putting a marketing plan together, you must focus on the type of market you are entering. Here are some guiding questions to answer in your marketing plan:

- What is the supply and demand for my products and/or services?
- Is this particular market expanding or declining?
- How will I capitalize on this venture?
- After researching your potential customer base, who is your target market? Include ages, gender, and geographic location.
- Who is my competition?
- What is my competitive edge?
- What is my ideal pricing structure? How much above wholesale am I willing to go?

You will need to address all of these questions in your marketing plan and business plan. If you are not skilled in this area, consider employing a marketing specialist.

5

Play by the Rules

Warren Buffett and Bernie Madoff are two of the most recognizable names in American business history. One is a beacon of integrity, a leader now in his nineties who continues to operate a company that is so profitable and admired that Berkshire Hathaway's annual meetings draw thousands of shareholders and investors. The other was disgraced and died in prison, burdened by the knowledge that he cost thousands of people billions of dollars (for some, their life's savings), and that his actions led to the suicide of his oldest son.

For me, Buffett illustrates the truth that in today's fast-paced business world it is possible to build a business and live a life of honesty and integrity, even when everyone else is seemingly trying to make it to the top by playing fast and loose with the truth as they bend the rules. As *CBS MoneyWatch* reporter Margaret Heffernan once noted:

> When Warren Buffett looks for companies to buy, he looks for two qualities in the CEO: energy and integrity. The benefits of energy are obvious – every entrepreneur and leader needs stamina to keep going through tough times and take advantage of good ones. What's more intriguing about Buffett's second requirement - integrity - is the way he defines it: The ability to say "no."[1]

However, while these two qualities are essential elements of a skilled CEO, they should be integral to every person who hopes to achieve success. As Buffet has said:

> Somebody once said that in looking for people to hire, you look for these three qualities: integrity, intelligence, and energy. And if you don't have the first, the other two will kill you. You think about it; it's true. If you hire somebody without [integrity], you really want them to be dumb and lazy.[2]

The polar opposite of Berkshire Hathaway's chairman is Madoff. The founder of a Wall Street investment firm, he was also at one time non-executive chairman of the nation's first electronic stock quotations system. Madoff took what had been a legitimate investment firm and turned its asset management division into a dishonest scheme. As with all devious systems that create the illusion of handsome returns by paying old investors with funds invested by newcomers, this house of cards ultimately collapsed. Investors lost $20 billion.

Caught in December of 2008 and charged with fraud, money laundering, perjury, and theft, Madoff went to prison in 2009 after a judge handed him a 150-year sentence. Even now, only a few of his victims have regained their losses. In writing about Madoff, business reporter Stephanie Yang noted the name for his ruse originated with Charles Ponzi, a 1920s-era swindler who promised 50 percent returns on investments in only ninety days.

Such schemes are run by a central operator, who uses the money from new, incoming investors to pay promised returns to older ones, Yang wrote. She explained how this makes the operation seem profitable and legitimate despite the absence of monetary returns. Meanwhile, the person running the scheme either pockets the extra money or uses it to expand the operation. To avoid having too many investors reclaim their "profits," Ponzi schemes encourage them to stay in the game and earn even more money. The "investing strategies" used are vague and /or secretive, which schemers claim is to protect their business. Then all they need to do is tell investors how much they are making periodically, without actually providing any real returns.

> Ponzi schemes aren't usually very sustainable. The setup eventually falls apart after: (1) The operator takes the remaining investment money and runs. (2) New investors become harder to find, meaning the flow of cash dies out. (3) Too many current investors begin to pull out and request their returns.
>
> In Madoff's case, things began to deteriorate after clients requested a total of $7 billion back in returns. Unfortunately for Madoff, he only had $200 million to $300 million left to give.[3]

As Madoff's Ponzi scheme shows, every house of cards will eventually collapse.

The Big Question

From the age we develop a workable understanding of our surroundings until we get old and die, all of us face the age-old dilemma: Should I play by the rules or cheat to get ahead? After all, those who think nothing of cutting a few corners say things like:

- ❖ "Good guys finish last."
- ❖ "Rules are made to be broken."
- ❖ "The ends justify the means."

I'm sure you've heard these or similar rationalizations. Indeed, statements like this are so common they can easily worm their way into your thinking and justify thoughts that "no one will get hurt" if you cheat a little. Yet following the rules will reap dividends. Having played by the rules for more than thirty years in business, I see them as an ironclad route to success. Regardless of how others try to justify their cheating or how far they seem to advance, honesty pays.

Business Smart *Principle*

Every person who proclaims himself or herself a Christian business owner is bound by honor and obedience to God's Word.

However, beyond that, disregarding the rules is a ticket to anarchy, disillusionment, and disaster.

When I think of rules, I see them falling into three primary categories: legal, societal, and self-imposed. The Bible speaks plainly to legal rules in this passage from Romans:

> Let every soul be subject to the governing authorities. For there is no authority except from God, and the authorities that exist are appointed by God. Therefore whoever resists the authority resists the ordinance of God, and those who resist will bring

judgment on themselves. For rulers are not a terror to good works, but to evil. Do you want to be unafraid of the authority? Do what is good, and you will have praise from the same.

- Romans 13:1-3

Legal rules are black and white. We live in a country of laws and rules. The rule is simple: don't break the law. The Bible spells out laws too, with the original form handed down to Moses on Mount Sinai. The Ten Commandments are also black and white. The rule is: don't break them. Sooner or later, those who violate the rules (whether those in the Bible or the law of the land) will get caught and receive the proper consequences. Those who play by the rules in business will get their just rewards.

Societal rules are a bit more complex than legal rules. They involve sticky issues (such as ethics and morality) and tend to call for far more subjective judgments. Societal rules leave an individual to use his or her moral compass to guide their decisions. Such situations feature widely varying circumstances that often take a more subjective perspective. This moral compass is another component of *The God Factor*.

Many of us will break societal rules from time to time and feel bad about our actions. Yet we may shrug it off by saying, "Well, I'm not perfect" or "I'm only human," even though our actions may cause pain to others.

Then there are self-imposed rules, which are rules we place on ourselves. We often hear them expressed in religious circles, the workplace, and business. People verbalize them in such was as:

- ❖ "I won't compromise my principles to get to the top."
- ❖ "I don't play politics at work or church to get the position."
- ❖ "I won't work for a dishonest boss."
- ❖ "I won't do it because it's outside my comfort level."

Every sport features rules the competitors must follow. Failing to play by these rules will either earn a penalty or disqualify a person from the game. The same is true in business. Many people fail in business, not because they did not work hard or because they did not get an opportunity to succeed, but because they failed to play by the rules. Playing by the rules requires integrity and honesty.

How can an individual achieve success? With the qualities I outlined in talking about Warren Buffett: integrity and honesty. These are the most needed qualities for success, whether it involves business, church, education, government, or family. Integrity and honesty not only establish the foundation of success, but they are also the glue that holds people together in any type of relationship. After all, it doesn't matter how noble or worthwhile your cause, if you haven't earned people's trust by exhibiting integrity and trustworthiness, no one will listen to you.

Play by the Rules in the Marketplace

Joseph followed the rules of the marketplace. For example, he avoided intimate relations with another man's wife. After his ten jealous brothers first plotted to kill him before selling him into slavery, Joseph wound up in Egypt. There he wisely managed the house of his master, Potiphar. Because God was with Joseph, everything he did prospered. Potiphar promoted him to overseer of his home and all that Potiphar owned. Although now in a position of power, what Joseph faced next is an apt reminder that positions of power also bring incredible responsibilities, pressures, and temptations:

> And it came to pass after these things that his master's wife cast longing eyes on Joseph, and she said, "Lie with me." But he refused and said to his master's wife, "Look, my master does not know what is with me in the house, and he has committed all that he has to my hand. There is no one greater in this house than I, nor has he kept back anything from me but you, because you are his wife. How then can I do this great wickedness, and sin against God?"
>
> - Genesis 39:7–9

Joseph understood what the Bible says about adultery and not coveting your neighbor's wife. Not to mention his need to avoid violating the high level of trust his master had placed in him. His integrity allowed him to take a stand against disloyalty and dishonesty. Conversely, how many great leaders have fallen to sensual temptations? Whether religious, political, educational, military, or business leaders, their names could fill a book. Let us adopt the role model of Joseph to be *Business Smart*.

Play by the Rules Towards Public Property

Samuel is a prime example of someone who played by the rules towards public property by exhibiting integrity and honesty. As the presiding high priest of Israel for decades, he could have bent the rules to enrich himself. Yet during his long years of service, he maintained high standards when it came to public property:

> Now Samuel said to all Israel: "Indeed I have heeded your voice in all that you said to me, and have made a king over you. And now here is the king, walking before you; and I am old and grayheaded, and look, my sons are with you. I have walked before you from my childhood to this day. Here I am. Witness against me before the LORD and before His anointed: Whose ox have I taken, or whose donkey have I taken, or whom have I cheated? Whom have I oppressed, or from whose hand have I received any bribe with which to blind my eyes? I will restore it to you." And they said, "You have not cheated us or oppressed us, nor have you taken anything from any man's hand."
> - 1 Samuel 12:1-4

By contrast, how many athletes, movie stars, or business and political leaders would be willing to come before the public and ask for an open investigation of their lives? In the modern era, it seems stretching the truth and flaunting the standards many proclaim to uphold are a way of life instead of an exception. It takes men and women of integrity and honesty to open themselves to public scrutiny.

Why Some Small Businesses Make a Killing and Others Fail

Honesty Pays

At the start of this chapter, I discussed Warren Buffett and Bernie Madoff, whose integrity (or lack of it) has touched millions inside and outside of the business world. Integrity also matters in countless other arenas. When it comes to integrity in Christian circles, I automatically think of longtime evangelist Billy Graham. Throughout more than nine decades of life, Graham has demonstrated what it means to be a man of integrity. As Graham puts it:

> Many people ask, what is integrity? It means a person is the same on the inside as he or she claims to be on the outside. A man of integrity can be trusted. He is the same person alone in a hotel room a thousand miles from home as he is at work in his community or with his family. We have seen the tragic results of moral breakdown and shattered trust in people – from leaders in business and government to well-known sports figures, to husbands, wives, and families and, yes even the church. The erosion of basic moral and spiritual values seems to be getting more serious at every level of society. We are waking up to the fact that we are paying a terrible price for corruption in government and business – all testify that something is wrong. It's easy to point the finger at prominent people accused of corruption. We can easily see their sins and the results. But a careful look reveals that the same poison of self-gratification and greed exists in our hearts as well."[4]

While Graham practiced what he preached, in my mind an example of the opposite is Ted Haggard, the one-time leader of a Colorado Springs megachurch. He resigned from his church and as president of the National Association of Evangelicals after admitting to a homosexual affair and drug use. Three years later, Haggard confessed to a second inappropriate relationship with a twenty-year-old male volunteer from his church. The male told CNN: "(Haggard) used to say to me, 'You know what, Grant, you can become a man of God, and you can have a little bit of fun on the side.'"[5]

Although I recognize that Haggard has since worked to turn around his life, we cannot ignore the existence of this kind of statement. I believe so many have been deceived by such messages that it has translated into a rationalization that has infected many in the church. Namely, adopting the outlook that *not* playing by the rules is acceptable.

Sports is another arena where playing by the rules is vital. The examples set by athletes carry over into many other arenas. Two examples of integrity are former New York Yankees Derek Jeter and Mariano Rivera, who are both now retired. Commenting on Jeter's integrity, discipline, and consummate professionalism, one blogger wrote:

> He retired after 20 years without so much as a blemish on his character. Jeter was a hometown hero in New York and clearly one of the most popular, recognizable, successful (and wealthy) men in sports, yet managed to steer clear of the foolishness and temptation and bad behavior way too many

athletes (whether it be because of greed, ego, sense of entitlement or just plain ignorance) allow to senselessly ruin their lives.[6]

As for Rivera, after he retired, he renovated a long-vacant church just north of New York City where his wife, Clara, now serves as senior pastor. At the dedication ceremony, the legendary relief pitcher said:

> "Well I mean a baseball field is one thing, we've won championships and the world was different. And I thank God for that, because it was amazing - what we accomplished in baseball. But this is totally in a different level."[7]

There are numerous examples of athletes whose actions have disgraced their names. One current name is Tom Brady, the Super-Bowl-winning quarterback whose legacy has been tarnished by allegations of cheating. Lance Armstrong gained fame as a world class cyclist but wound up disgraced for his cheating, lying, and bullying. Golfer Tiger Woods worked to recover his prowess after adultery led to the collapse of his marriage. Ryan Braun won the National League's Most Valuable Player award for 2011, and then got suspended midway through the 2013 season after admitting he had used performance enhancing drugs.

Living by the Truth

In a society where so many people are living in moral failure, it is no wonder we see degenerating standards in business, the home, church, and school. Lying and cheating have become so commonplace it may leave you wondering if it is even possible to live by truth. Yet, before someone can live by the truth, he or she must understand it. The dictionary says that truth can be defined as conformity to fact. It is extremely important to set a standard of truth in our lives that is never negotiable. As the bedrock on which integrity is built, truth must become a habitual practice in every *Business Smart* endeavor. Truth isn't according to the way I see it, but according to facts.

There is great power in the truth, which is why Jesus told His followers: "And you shall know the truth, and the truth shall make you free" (John 8:32). When we walk in truth it will never let us down. We don't have to struggle later to remember what we said about a matter because we know we didn't lie. When we are truthful, we can open ourselves up with transparency for all to see. Truth exposes darkness and protects us from deception. When we abide in truth, we won't have to guess what today's standards are—they are the same they were yesterday. We must fight against every thought or reasoning that is opposed to the truth, following the advice Paul gave to the church at Corinth: "We demolish arguments and every pretension that sets itself up against the knowledge of God, and we take captive every thought to make it obedient to Christ" (2 Corinthians 10:5 NIV).

Given the prevalence of lying in the modern age, many ask, "Why do so many people lie?" Since I am not a psychologist, I won't presume to explore the psychological factors for such behavior, but here are some basic reasons I think are behind it:

- ❖ **Fear**

  Fear is a prime reason for lying. A man may lie to get a job because he is afraid that if he tells the truth, he will get passed over. Others lie to climb the ladder or escape the consequences of their actions.

- ❖ **Pride**

  Pride lets us think more highly of ourselves than we should. Some lie in an attempt to "polish" their image.

- ❖ **Ignorance**

  This is nothing more than a lack of knowledge. People sometimes lie because although they know they do not have all the information they need, they would rather pretend they do (an action also rooted in pride).

The Truth Hurts

Ephesians 4:15 teaches us to speak the truth in love. Since telling the truth can sometimes cause others pain, or make them angry because they don't like their flaws or hypocrisy exposed, it is easy to avoid telling the truth or even engage in lying. The truth hurts because of ego. The truth hurts because the reality of my truth might be different from another person's viewpoint of the truth.

Are you playing by the rules of integrity and honesty? Here's a checklist to examine if you are practicing *Business Smart* principles:

- ✓ Am I accountable? Who do I trust to tell me the truth about myself?

- ✓ Am I willing to confront hidden bad habits and weaknesses?
- ✓ Am I deceiving myself that I am playing by the rules when I am not?
- ✓ Do I think I am better than everyone else?
- ✓ Am I honest when no one else is looking?
- ✓ Am I lying to prove my worth?
- ✓ Am I telling half-truths because of fear?
- ✓ Am I compromising the principles I say I believe in to get ahead?
- ✓ Do I give false reports about others in order to make myself look good?

If you are committed to play by the rules, you must answer these questions honestly, just as David did:

> For I acknowledge my transgressions, and my sin *is* always before me. Against You, You only, have I sinned, and done this evil in Your sight – that You may be found just when You speak, and blameless when You judge. Behold, I was brought forth in iniquity, and in sin my mother conceived me.
>
> - Psalm 51:3-5

We must arrive at a similar place of honesty and integrity. Whenever we find deception, false pride, or other worldly goals motivating our actions, we must be willing to say, "I have done wrong." Let us humble ourselves and come face to face with the truth. Decide today to play by the rules in business, the home, church, and school. Avoid lying and deception. Walk in truth in all areas of life. Then you will succeed.

6

Work Hard

Business Smart Principle
"He who has a slack hand becomes poor, but the hand of the diligent makes rich."
- Proverbs 10:4

If you are, or plan to be, a business owner and have not made a quality decision to work hard—just forget it. Sustainable success is not *just* gonna happen without hard work.

Day after day when I was young, I watched my father stride through the front door following the midnight shift at a Jamaican sugar cane factory. After chatting with us over breakfast, when we left for school at eight o'clock, he went to work in the fields, raising the food needed to feed our family. Such a grueling routine might break the spirit of a lesser person. In similar, high-pressure circumstances some escape through a bottle of liquor or head out the door while leaving the state to assume their responsibilities. Not my father. He toiled diligently to put me, eight sisters, and three brothers through school. Growing up I never lacked adequate food, clothing, and a roof over my head.

I am so thankful that my parents taught me a good work ethic! No matter what the setbacks, obstacles, or financial strains, I knew that one secret to enduring came from diligence. More than once I asked my father why he worked such long hours. In response he always told me about the life of Jesus, often commenting, "Jesus was the hardest-working man who ever lived on this earth." Those words burrowed deep into my spirit. Today, they help me strive for success.

The alternative to diligent effort can be seen on the streets of major metropolitan cities and small towns alike. Namely, people drifting through life aimlessly while hoping the government, a lottery ticket, or someone else's hard work will somehow bring them the good fortune they crave—all with little or no effort on their part. The chances of this happening are akin to finding a grain of salt on a sandy ocean beach. I have always liked the way Solomon puts it: "He who has a slack hand becomes poor, but the hand of the diligent makes rich" (Proverbs 10:4).

Yet somehow, millions manage to disregard this wisdom, looking at work as a curse that God handed to Adam and Eve in the Garden of Eden, or a necessary evil that will vanish once they make it to heaven. This is a skewed view of work, which is an expression of God's nature, character, and creative ability. Work is a worthwhile endeavor that produces a sense of accomplishment and brings intrinsic personal satisfaction and a monetary surplus that we can use to help others. Yet for some, the questions remain:

- ❖ In today's face-paced world, how should we view work?
- ❖ Is it necessary to work hard to achieve success?
- ❖ Is hard work a necessary evil?

The answer: It depends on one's perspective.

Throughout my life I have heard such statements as, "Don't work yourself too hard," and, "Take it easy and enjoy life a little." Although often well-intentioned (and you can cross the line into becoming a workaholic who neglects family and other responsibilities), these remarks can have a negative impact when it comes to pondering decisions about work. Many of us face continuing challenges as we contemplate the value of work, how hard we should work, and when we should relax to devote time to other concerns.

Indeed, the way we decide these questions will have a huge impact on our success. In order to answer them correctly, we must know what the Bible says about hard work and its opposite—laziness. I have used the Bible's principles on diligence to shape my attitude towards work and my superiors. As a result, I have reaped the rewards.

Work Hard - Work Smart: The Meaning of Hard Work

The phrase, *hard work*, can evoke all kinds of images. Because of their background, some people think of it as manual labor demanding they work all day in the hot sun, sweating and generating callused hands. Others may think of standing for hours on end, checking out goods at a register; staring at a computer screen; or staying up late at night to finish the myriad of details related to a business trip.

The Bible defines hard work in fairly simple, straightforward terms: "The hand of the diligent will rule, but the lazy man will be put to forced labor" (Proverbs 12:24). In other words, hard work is defined as *diligence*. It is not only how many hours we put in on the job, or how many calluses appear on our hands, but our diligence that makes the difference. How faithful are we to the task? How efficiently do we apply what we know to what we do? Do we go the extra mile in an effort to be the best we can be, or are we satisfied with doing the bare minimum? The latter is personified by those I've heard say, in an effort to excuse their slothfulness: "Good enough for government work."

Biblical Principles of Hard Work

❖ **God is a Hard Worker**

The book of Genesis offers a portrait of a hard-working, diligent Lord. In addition to creating the heavens and the earth in six days, "The LORD God planted a garden eastward in Eden, and there He put the man whom He had formed" (Genesis 2:8).

The foundation of work begins with an appreciation for our Creator's example. God did not fold His hands and wait for a garden to grow. Instead, He made man, placed him in the garden that He had planted, and gave Adam the assignment "to tend and keep it" (see Genesis 2:15). These passages reveal the necessity of work, which offers the only sure escape from a hard life. Indeed, they reveal that God intended for men and women to work diligently and efficiently. Since God is a hard worker, He honors hard workers and approves of their labors. As the psalmist put it: "And may the Lord our God show us his approval and make our efforts successful. Yes, make our efforts successful!" (Psalm 90:17 NLT).

Not only does God intend for us to work, He wants us to gain fulfillment and happiness from our efforts. This is why He gave us Himself as an example to follow. Work must become a major factor in our lives if we ever expect to hold the keys to personal fulfillment and financial security. It is God's pleasure to bless the diligent. He takes pleasure in the work of our hands. He gave us His promise that He will bless the work of our hands. Moses expressed this best when he reminded the children of Israel before they crossed into the Promised Land: "For the LORD your God has blessed you in everything you have done" (Deuteronomy 2:7 NLT).

Yet, even as we work hard, we must remember to keep a balance in life and not let work consume every waking hour. Just as He set the example of working diligently, God took time to rest from His labors: "And on the seventh day God ended His work which He had done, and He rested on the seventh day from all His work which He had done" (Genesis 2:2).

God is so serious about rest that He made keeping the Sabbath one of the Ten Commandments and expounded on it in greater detail than with any of the others:

> Remember the Sabbath day, to keep it holy. Six days you shall labor and do all your work, but the seventh day is the Sabbath of the LORD your God. In it you shall do no work: you, nor your son, nor your daughter, nor your male servant, nor your female servant, nor your cattle, nor your stranger who is within your gates. For in six days the LORD made the heavens and the earth, the sea, and all that is in them, and rested the seventh day. Therefore the LORD blessed the Sabbath day and hallowed it.
>
> - Exodus 20:8-11

In other words, God wants us to work but He also wants us to:

- ✓ Rest and enjoy life
- ✓ Spend time with Him in worship
- ✓ Spend time with family and friends
- ✓ Take some time for ourselves

Without hard work, a person's life becomes shallow. Success means maintaining a balance between work, family, worship, and pleasure.

❖ Jesus was a Hard Worker

A study of the life of Jesus will quickly reveal He constantly worked. As He declared to His disciples before healing a man who was blind from birth: "I must work the works of him that sent me, while it is day; the night cometh, when no man can work" (John 9:4 KJV). When Jesus healed a man on the Sabbath and upset the religious leaders who cared more about tradition than helping people, He made no excuses. Instead, He told His critics: "My Father has been working until now, and I have been working" (John 5:17). Likewise, when Jesus was separated from His family at the age of twelve, Mary and Joseph came looking for Him. His parents were upset because it took them three days to find Him. When Mary and Joseph located Him, He was in the temple, Jesus answered simply: "Why did you seek Me? Did you not know that I must be about My Father's business?" (Luke 2:49).

Although only twelve years old when He asked this question, Jesus poses a timeless inquiry for all of us: *Are we carrying out our Father's business?* Jesus let nothing stop Him from doing His work. Even if you haven't followed this principle in years past, you can start today.

Not only was Jesus hard at work as a young man, He later praised the value of initiative and effort when He told the parable of the talents. In this story, He described a master going on a long journey. Before leaving, he called together three servants and entrusted them with his money because he expected them to increase it and make a profit. When he returned, he asked the servants to give an account of what they did. The first two reported an increase; the servant who received five talents had doubled them. The servant given two talents also doubled them. The master rewarded both for their work. The moral of the story is Christ's affirmation; *hard work will lead to success.*

By contrast, the third servant did nothing with the money he received, excusing his inaction by telling the master:

> "Lord, I knew you to be a hard man, reaping where you have not sown, and gathering where you have not scattered seed. And I was afraid, and went and hid your talent in the ground. Look, there you have what is yours."
>
> - Matthew 25:24-25

Everyone who thinks they can slough off or only slide by with the barest of efforts should study the master's response to the servant:

> But his lord answered and said to him, "You wicked and lazy servant, you knew that I reap where I have not sown, and gather where I have

not scattered seed. So you ought to have deposited my money with the bankers, and at my coming I would have received back my own with interest. So take the talent from him, and give it to him who has ten talents. For to everyone who has, more will be given, and he will have abundance; but from him who does not have, even what he has will be taken away. And cast the unprofitable servant into the outer darkness. There will be weeping and gnashing of teeth."

- Matthew 25:26–30

God does not smile on lackadaisical slothful attitudes. Indeed, the third servant earned the label of "wicked and lazy" and the severe punishment of being cast into outer darkness. Remember the outcome of this story whenever you are tempted to be lazy or indifferent. This unprofitable servant was not ignorant of his master's expectations. Neither should we be ignorant of our heavenly Master's expectation that we work hard.

❖ Jacob was a Hard Worker

This Old Testament patriarch is the epitome of hard work. Through Jacob's example, we can see when a person learns to work hard, it will be easy to pay the price to receive what they love. With hard work you can achieve anything you want, no matter what it costs. Jacob, who loved Rachel, declared to her father, Laban, that he would work seven years for her (see Genesis 29). Since Jacob did not have the cash to pay the customary dowry, he gave his labor instead. Although Laban cheated him by giving him his older daughter, Leah, as a bride, Jacob agreed to work another seven years to win Rachel's hand. Jacob chose to do so because he was a hard worker.

The Benefits of Hard Work in Business

Success is never accidental. When you work hard, success will follow. This is why Solomon wrote: "Do you see someone skilled in their work? They will serve before kings; they will not serve before officials of low rank" (Proverbs 22:29 NIV). When you work with excellence, the only limits on what you can become are those you place on yourself. Those willing to pay the price of hard work can achieve great things.

This is the point of the story of the tribes of Ephraim and Manasseh, who sought more land when Israel crossed into the Promised Land:

> Then the children of Joseph spoke to Joshua, saying, "Why have you given us only one lot and one share to inherit, since we are a great people, inasmuch as the LORD has blessed us until now?" So Joshua answered them, "If you are a great people, then go up to the forest country and clear a place for yourself there in the land of the Perizzites and the giants, since the mountains of Ephraim are too confined for you. … You are a great people and have great power; you shall not have only one lot, but the mountain country shall be yours. Although it is wooded, you shall cut it down, and its farthest extent shall be yours; for you shall drive out the Canaanites, though they have iron chariots and are strong."
>
> — Joshua 17:14–15 and 17–18

This passage illustrates how the work of one's hands is their channel of promotion and prosperity. The hands of the slacker hold no future, for the main choice is between work and a hard life. By choosing work, you can be freed from a hard life. Unfortunately, some people choose idleness and the lazy route through life. Those who refuse to work will end up in chains, reduced to begging for their existence. There is never disgrace in hard work—only honor.

Five Principles of Hard Work

From experience, I have learned five key principles of hard work, as well as five enemies of hard work that you should avoid. I have used these key principles to achieve success. When you follow them, they will help you to become a highly effective worker in any occupation or field of endeavor; especially when building a sustainable business.

1. Maintain Focus

I discovered this principle while studying Joshua:

> This Book of the Law shall not depart from your mouth, but you shall meditate in it day and night, that you may observe to do according to all that is written in it. For then you will make your way prosperous, and then you will have good success.
>
> - Joshua 1:8

God told Joshua to meditate "day and night" on His Word so that Joshua would know what to do. The principle of focus will carry you far, because it will help you avoid distractions in a world filled with distractions. Have you ever watched a couple in a restaurant who spent more time watching their smartphones than each other? It is tough to carry on a conversation with another person when you don't focus on him or her. When you fail to focus on God's Law and its principles of discipline, honesty, diligence, and hard work, you will get swept away by all the "noise" of modern life.

As part of this principle, you must set clear, defined goals. Don't let anything deter you from reaching them. This is the point of God's message to Joshua:

> Only be strong and very courageous, that you may observe to do according to all the law which Moses My servant commanded you; do not turn from it to the right hand or to the left, that you may prosper wherever you go.
>
> - Joshua 1:7

In other words, you must know exactly what the task is about. You must have a clear understanding of what you are about to do or want to do. Achieving focus calls for understanding, which comes from having a well-written plan. When you don't understand what you are about to do, you lose focus and become uninterested in the task. This is why God told Joshua to focus on the law day and night until he understood it. Working hard while lacking focus will only lead to frustration. Focus and concentration go hand in hand. Staying single-minded is the key to getting things done.

Business Smart *Principle*

F.O.C.U.S.
Follow One Course Until Success

2. Get to Work Early

For my business to thrive in a fast-paced world, I adopted a principle that gives me a competitive advantage, and will help you too. Show up an hour early every day for work and you will be surprised at how much more you can get done. An early start helps you get organized and avoid distractions as the day progresses. Setting out a plan for the day will also help you stay focused.

3. Stay Late

Staying late at work also helped me succeed. It allows me to review the work I accomplished during the day and measure my output. The first chapter of Genesis reveals the pattern God followed: He worked a complete day, in the morning and the evening, and completed what He started that day.

Staying late will give you a head start on tomorrow, too. If you haven't quite finished the list of tasks you had hoped to complete during the day, you will know what to put on the top of your priority list for the next day. Practice the principle of staying late and you will gain a competitive advantage on those who are always checking the clock so they can rush for the exits at quitting time.

4. Finish What You Start

Set and keep deadlines, whether for a major project or a small job you need to finish. When you set deadlines, it will force you to work harder and with more focus. A job or a task without a deadline usually ends in futility because it lacks a motivational force. Thus, it has no emergency for closure—and never gets done. It is a good practice to promise other people when you will finish. When you promise someone else a completion date, it will motivate you to finish on time.

What would've happened if God didn't set deadlines on each day to complete what He started? In Genesis 1, God started making light, and He completed that task in one day before moving on to the next. This stands in stark contrast to those who are plagued with "almost there" syndrome. Every task they start reaches a point of "almost finished" but never quite makes it. During my years in the marketplace and in ministry, I have repeatedly heard such statements as:

- ❖ "I almost got the job."
- ❖ "I almost bought the home."
- ❖ "I almost finished college."

Those who expect to succeed need to practice finishing whatever they start.

5. Use Diligence

Diligence is not just working hard but sticking with the task. In life, you will sometimes tackle jobs that are very time-consuming, emotionally draining, and filled with conflict. Some offer so many twists and turns and revisions that only with diligence will you stick with it until it is done right. Practicing diligence is a necessary ingredient of success.

Five Enemies of Hard Work

You might wonder why I chose such a strong word as *enemies* of hard work. In this context, the following obstacles will prevent you from reaching your desires or goals and stifle your hopes of success. Therefore, no matter how innocent or innocuous they may seem, they stand in direct opposition to you. They are your enemies.

1. Working with a Slack Hand

Solomon advised people to never settle for lazy half-hearted efforts in life: "The soul of a lazy man desires, and has nothing; but the soul of the diligent shall be made rich" (Proverbs 13:4). Now, many people will automatically consider how much money they can earn from hard work, but a "slack hand" refers to many areas of life, not just money. Take the divorce rate. How many originate with a "slack hand" in marriage? As one who has suffered the sting of divorce, I am not criticizing those who have been, nor saying every case is because of this. Yet I have seen far too many divorces stem from laziness. Namely, the spouses refuse to do the hard work required to have a good marriage.

The same happens on the job. Granted, during the economic downturn that started in 2008, millions lost their jobs because of forces beyond their control. Yet I regularly encounter people who have lost their job because they put forth a minimum of effort and spent more time around the water cooler than their desk. People who are dealing with a slack hand always want to take it easy. Often, when I am working hard on a project, people will stop by to offer such comments as, "Take it easy," or, "Don't work too hard." I reply, "I am taking it hard!" Meaning I am taking it hard so I can beat the spirit of a slack hand.

2. Procrastination

How many times do people fail in life—not because they aren't qualified but because they keep putting off what needs to get done today until tomorrow or the day after? As a father, husband, pastor, and business owner, I come across many qualified people who never achieved success because of their habit of putting off a difficult task until the last minute. Then they either fail to complete it or make mistakes in their rush to finish it.

3. Complainers

Complainers never get the job done; if you hang around complainers, they will stop you from getting your work done too. Complainers are like dump trucks: their mind is full of trash. They are always beset by problems. They live from problem to problem. Life never works for them. Life is too hard. Not only is it too hard, they love to tell others how hard it is. Every time you see a complainer, they will air the same set of grievances. Since complainers drain energy from you, you should avoid them so you can get back to work.

4. Talkers

In every workplace, there are talkers. Since they never run out of words, talkers never listen. They have an intrinsic beacon that enables them to find you when you are in the midst of a crucial task that requires intense focus. Limit the time you spend listening to them. Don't try to talk back or give advice, if you do, you won't get anything done. Remember, talkers are not workers, so limit your exposure and get back to work.

5. Interruptions

If you allow it, interruptions can be a way of life. In today's fast-paced world, some interruptions are unavoidable. Telephone, text messages, emails, faxes, family crises, or people stopping by are interruptions that many of you face on a daily basis. However, the way you deal with them will have a major impact on your success.

Here are some suggestions for dealing with interruptions:

- Use caller ID to screen calls and only answer if it is your boss, spouse, or children; a customer; or a client calling. Otherwise, let voicemail do its job.
- Pick a specific time each day to check voicemail and prioritize the important ones that require a response.
- When possible, use email to communicate. This can help avoid extended conversations that distract from the workday.
- Avoid constant text messaging. Many are not on your high priority list and don't need an immediate response. Only answer priority messages and let the rest linger until the evening or the weekend.
- While some see them as outdated, a fax is another way to get a message out quickly. Let your fax machine work for you, not against you.
- These strategies will help you to minimize interruptions, thereby maximizing your effectiveness.

7

The Power of Unrelenting Courage

The power of unrelenting courage is a *must* to confront the *Fear of Failure*. Perseverance, determination, and willpower fuel successful *Business Smart* entrepreneurs to pass the test of time.

Climbing the ladder of success in today's fast-paced world of business requires unrelenting courage. Life offers too many setbacks, too many disappointments, too many frustrations, and too many dead-end alleys for the faint of heart. Climbing the ladder means taking one step at a time while recognizing each step gets progressively tougher. Building a business requires unrelenting courage to beat the *Fear of Failure*.

People like Noah Galloway are a great example of what it takes to overcome obstacles. This native of Birmingham, Alabama, was assigned to the 1st Battalion of the 502nd Infantry of the 101st Airborne Division out of Fort Campbell, Kentucky, during Operation Iraqi Freedom.

Just three months into his second tour of duty, he experienced a life-changing injury. On December 19, 2005, the sergeant lost his left arm above the elbow and his left leg above the knee in an IED (improvised explosive device) attack. Transported to Germany for medical treatment, Galloway remained unconscious for five days. When he woke up late in the evening on Christmas Eve, he learned that he had lost two of his limbs and sustained severe injuries to his right leg and his jaw. Once doctors there stabilized him, the military transferred him to Walter Reed Army Medical Center in Washington, DC.

"After a long stint in recovery and rehabilitation, Galloway did what many disabled veterans do, becoming withdrawn, out of shape and depressed," his website says.

The former fitness fanatic and hyper competitive athlete was now drinking, smoking, and sleeping his days away. But late one night, Galloway took a long look in the mirror and realized there was more to him than the injuries. And he set a goal to get back in shape, be healthier, and inspire others.

"Now a personal trainer and motivational speaker, Galloway doesn't take excuses from his clients, fans and followers—and finds ways to get things done. He continues to compete (in sporting events), participating in adventure races around the country, such as Tough Mudder, Spartan events, and Crossfit competitions, plus numerous 5K and 10K races."[1]

In 2015, Noah appeared on *Dancing with the Stars: Season 20* with his partner Shana Burgess, a spirited dancer from Australia. His unrelenting courage appeared on national TV, night after night, until they reached the finals. Although they didn't win, they finished third, and Noah captured millions of hearts with his display of courage. I cheered for him too, because Noah showed the kind of courage that God calls for from His people.

Unrelenting courage overcomes the *Fear of Failure* and is another essential component of *The God Factor*. Both are necessary to build, maintain, and advance a *Business Smart* endeavor. Unrelenting courage is reflected in the Lord's command to Joshua, as Israel's leader prepared to enter the Promised Land:

> Be strong and of good courage, for to this people you shall divide as an inheritance the land which I swore to their fathers to give them. Only be strong and very courageous . . .
>
> - Joshua 1:6–7

The same words apply to those hoping to succeed in the twenty-first century. It will take unrelenting courage to overcome insurmountable odds in business.

The Power of Courage

It is not possible to have the unrelenting courage we need to overcome the *Fear of Failure* without perseverance, determination, and willpower. Without these attributes, victory would not be possible. For men and women who consistently and intentionally apply these traits to confront and overcome the *Fear of Failure,* anything is possible. They will propel themselves to great achievements.

A good example is Mary Kay Ash. She used unrelenting courage to overcome the *Fear of Failure* when she saw the need to start a company with her life savings of $5,000. Her attorney didn't believe in her dream and sent her this discouraging message: "If you are going to throw away your life savings, why don't you just put it directly in the trash can?"[2] Yet, thanks to the power of unrelenting courage, this savvy entrepreneur turned a small store in Dallas, Texas, with five products into an international network that brought her dream to life:

> That dream was to inspire women to transform their lives, and in doing so, help other women achieve success. Today, with 3.5 million independent beauty consultants, Mary Kay offers more than 200 . . . products in more than 35 countries around the world.
> . . . the Mary Kay business opportunity has helped women from Kansas to Kazakhstan, discover extra income, empowered choices and true beauty from the inside out.[3]

Long before she achieved success though, Mary Kay could have quit. Especially after the untimely deaths of two of her three husbands. Mary Kay had three children (Richard, Ben and Marylyn) with her first husband, J. Ben Rogers. The two divorced after Rogers returned from serving in World War II. Her second marriage to a chemist was brief; he died of a heart attack in 1963, just one month after their wedding. She married her third husband, Mel Ash, in 1966 and the couple stayed together until Mel's death in 1980.[4]

Yet losing three husbands isn't the only adversity she faced. At the age of twenty-one, Ash went to work as a salesperson for a home products company, hosting parties to encourage women to buy household items. She was so good at it that eventually another company hired her away. After a little over a decade, she quit in frustration after watching a man whom she had trained get promoted above her, and at a much higher salary. So, in 1963 at the age of forty-five, in an era when far fewer women worked outside the home, Ash purchased the formulas for skin lotions from another family. Then she opened her store and started the business that would go on to employ more than 1.6 million people around the world.

Mary Kay is a pioneer for women in business. She built Mary Kay, Inc.'s global wholesale market to $4 billion in sales.[5] I can say without a doubt that this woman possessed the power of courage!

Standing Firm in Difficult Times

One leader who displayed unrelenting courage to overcome the *Fear of Failure* in one of the toughest crises modern-day America has faced was New York Mayor Rudolph Giuliani. After the September 11, 2001, terrorist attacks on the World Trade Center, he proved he could stand firm in the most difficult of times. His resolve included overcoming a devastating bout with prostate cancer. In addition, he endured the embarrassment of a highly publicized extra-marital affair, followed by a separation from his wife. Minutes after the planes hit the World Trade Center, Mayor Giuliani was on the scene, bringing a scene of strength to the city. He stood firm when fear struck the hearts of many Americans, serving as a pillar of courage.

A corporate leader who also stood firm in the toughest of times is Fred Smith, who founded the Federal Express Corporation in 1971. During the mid-1960s, while attending Yale University, Smith wrote a term paper for an economics class on the need for reliable overnight delivery in a computerized, information age. Considering "FedEx" is a household name in much of the world, I can only chuckle when I read the comment his professor wrote on the paper: "The concept is interesting and well-formed, but in order to earn better than a 'C,' the idea must be feasible."[6]

Several years later, by combining unrelenting courage with innovative thinking, Smith used this "interesting but unfeasible" idea to launch the world's first overnight delivery company. It changed the courier industry forever. Yet, launching the company didn't mean smooth sailing. He invested $4 million he inherited from his father (the millionaire founder of Dixie Greyhound Bus Lines and Toddle House Restaurants) into the company in 1972, along with $80 million in loan and equity investments. Although initially slow, business soon picked up, spurring further expansion. Then the roof caved in, thanks to the Arab oil embargo.

Facing rapidly escalating fuel prices, by mid-1974 Federal Express was hemorrhaging more than $1 million a month. Smith asked investors for more money to keep the company afloat, but they refused. He didn't quit though, and eventually raised another $11 million. The company did not go down. In fact, by 1980, FedEx's revenues hit $415.4 million and profits rose to $38.7 million! Reflecting on those days, he said, "I was very committed to the people that had signed on with me, and if we were going to go down, we were going to go down with a fight. It wasn't going to be because I checked out and didn't finish."[7] Fred Smith's story is living proof that if you try once and fail, you should keep trying. Call on the power of unrelenting courage until you succeed.

For inspiration, you can also turn to a biblical example: the story of David and Goliath. The Philistine army came against Israel to engage in battle; the two armies faced each other on opposite sides of a steep valley. The Philistines' champion measured over nine feet tall. Protected by full body armor, Goliath came out day after day for forty days, mocking and challenging the Israelites to fight him. Afraid of the giant, King Saul and his army always ran away.

One day, a young shepherd named David approached the front lines to deliver food to his brother. During this time Goliath again came out to mock the men of Israel. After hearing his taunts, David asked, "What shall be done for the man who kills this Philistine and takes away the reproach from Israel? For who is this uncircumcised Philistine, that he should defy the armies of the living God?" (1 Samuel 17:26).

His brothers mocked him for even asking such a question. Saul told him that, as a youth, David was not able to face such a mighty warrior. David replied:

> "Your servant used to keep his father's sheep, and when a lion or a bear came and took a lamb out of the flock, I went out after it and struck it, and delivered the lamb from its mouth; and when it arose against me, I caught it by its beard, and struck and killed it. Your servant has killed both lion and bear; and this uncircumcised Philistine will be like one of them, seeing he has defied the armies of the living God." Moreover David said, "The LORD, who delivered me from the paw of the lion and from the paw of the bear, He will deliver me from the hand of

this Philistine." And Saul said to David, "Go, and the Lord be with you!"

- 1 Samuel 17:34–37

Imagine how the course of history would have changed without the determination demonstrated by this young man! David fought the giant and killed him. Many failed to respond to the challenge. However, David's reliance on intuitive prompting (namely, *The God Factor*) and combating the *Fear of Failure* with unrelenting courage, brought him and all of Israel great success.

7 Attributes of Unrelenting Courage Every Business Owner Must Possess:

Studying the attributes leaders with unrelenting courage display and committing to apply them to your life, puts you on the road to establishing a sustainable and profitable *Business Smart* enterprise.

1. Recognize Tests Never End

The stories I shared in this chapter have a common theme—that while great leaders go through different levels of testing, they never give up. Before David could kill Goliath, he faced the test of a lion attacking his sheep. David killed the lion. When a bear came to attack his sheep, he also killed the bear. David's next test came in the form of the giant, Goliath. You get the idea: *you will repeatedly face tests in life.* This is why you must possess the power of unrelenting courage to stand up to the tests, no matter how difficult they may seem.

Most people run away from these life tests. I believe it is because they are afraid of failure and, more to the point, the fear of embarrassment if they stumble and fall. I often ask would-be entrepreneurs this question: "What would you do if you believed you couldn't fail?" Then I add, "No one likes to fail, but we fail so that we can win." The next time you face a test, remember the stories of the great leaders I just reviewed.

2. Be Yourself

To be yourself, you must first know who you are. It is not easy to say "no" to people. I know, because as a father, husband, pastor, and business owner, saying "no" is difficult. My easy-going enthusiastic nature instinctively makes me want to ensure everyone's happiness. But saying "no" is sure to put a frown on someone's face. Yet I also know if I can't say what I know to be true, I wouldn't be true to myself and those around me.

Because David knew who he was, he wasn't afraid to declare that God would give him the strength, the courage, and the necessary weapons to bring down the giant who threatened the well-being of God's people. David knew who he was and the source of his strength. When you know who you are, it is much easier for you to say "no" if you are asked to be someone else.

3. Stand Strong in Your Convictions

David was a man of convictions. Like other leaders I have mentioned in this chapter, he demonstrated strong conviction to overcome obstacles and setbacks. When David's brothers tried to discourage him, he didn't give in:

> Now Eliab his oldest brother heard when he spoke to the men; and Eliab's anger was aroused against David, and he said, "Why did you come down here? And with whom have you left those few sheep in the wilderness? I know your pride and the insolence of your heart, for you have come down to see the battle." And David said, "What have I done now? Is there not a cause?"
>
> - 1 Samuel 17:28–29

Business $mart Principle

When there is a cause, you will not quit.

4. Maintain Your Desire to Triumph

Unrelenting courage is born out of the attribute of *desire*. You will always reach for what you desire. Desire drove David to face Goliath. Desire drove Fred Smith to build Federal Express Corporation into an international shipping company. Desire also drove Henry Ford to create an engine with all eight cylinders cast in one block. When an engineer who worked for him insisted it was impossible, Ford directed him to tell his department to continue until they succeeded. When the engineer again replied that it was impossible, Ford pressed the engineer to tell his department to continue. Finally, they succeeded in building a V-8 engine.[8]

Ford's unrelenting courage revolutionized the automotive industry. The strength of your desires will determine how far you will reach, and how far you reach cannot surpass your level of courage.

5. Pursue Your Goal Until It Becomes Reality

The proof of unrelenting courage is the continuation of the pursuit. Not every goal or task people pursue will become a reality. One can't pursue a goal or task to its fulfillment without unrelenting courage. You must fight a battle to win every crown. To be successful in life, you must respond to the challenges that try to turn you back from reaching your goal. Paul wisely advised his protégé, Timothy: "You therefore must endure hardship as a good soldier of Jesus Christ" (2 Timothy 2:3).

People of courage don't just wish to achieve, they pursue achievement. Pursuit is part of the hard work needed to succeed, and the willingness to work hard comes from unrelenting courage. You will never attain your goal without the courage to pursue it.

6. You Must Persevere

Perseverance is required to display unrelenting courage because you will only achieve your dream or goal at the end of a long quest; it will require long hours and hard work. As quoted by the prophet Habakkuk:

> For the vision is yet for an appointed time; but at the end it will speak, and it will not lie. Though it tarries, wait for it; because it will surely come, it will not tarry."
>
> - Habakkuk 2:3

No matter how worthwhile the goal or dream you are pursuing, you will encounter opportunities to fail in its pursuit. It takes perseverance, determination, and will power to activate the unrelenting courage required to be victorious over the *Fear of Failure* and see your dreams accomplished. While fighting discouragement and weariness, it helps to remember Paul's words to the Galatians: "Let us not become weary in doing good, for at the proper time we will reap a harvest if we do not give up" (Galatians 6:9 NIV).

Abraham Lincoln, the sixteenth president of the United States, is an example of perseverance. Whether in his business, personal life, or attempts to run for office, he failed nearly a dozen times. Among his setbacks were a failed business, a nervous breakdown, the death of a sweetheart, and defeats in the US Senate elections of 1854 and 1858. Yet he kept going until his election to the nation's highest office in the fall of 1861. Lincoln had a goal he was determined to fulfill, so he didn't give up. The *Fear of Failure* was unable to prevail over Lincoln's unrelenting courage to see his dream fulfilled. These qualities will also help you see your dream fulfilled.

7. Have Faith

The following passage is familiar to many Christians, but it bears repeating because its words are so true and personify the strong belief needed to possess unrelenting courage:

> Now faith is the substance of things hoped for, the evidence of things not seen. For by it the elders obtained a good testimony. By faith we understand that the worlds were framed by the word of God, so that the things which are seen were not made of things which are visible.
>
> - Hebrews 11:1-3

Why Some Small Businesses Make a Killing and Others Fail

One way to have this kind of faith is to read about the biblical heroes who demonstrated this quality, such as Abraham. The father of Israel was a man of unrelenting courage, driven by faith. Faith will keep you going against all odds. On a human level, Abraham and Sarah had lost all hope of having a child, but with faith, courage, and a promise from God, that belief stayed alive. Centuries later, Paul recalled:

> Therefore it is of faith that it might be according to grace, so that the promise might be sure to all the seed, not only to those who are of the law, but also to those who are of the faith of Abraham, who is the father of us all (as it is written, "I have made you a father of many nations") in the presence of Him whom he believed—God, who gives life to the dead and calls those things which do not exist as though they did; who, contrary to hope, in hope believed, so that he became the father of many nations, according to what was spoken, "So shall your descendants be."
> - Romans 4:16–18

There was no reason for Abraham and Sarah to hope for a child in their old age. After all, Abraham was a hundred years old and Sara was ninety. They had long ago passed the normal child-bearing age. All human reasoning opposed the very idea! Yet because of their strong belief in God's promise they believed. The application of biblical faith is more than a wish; it is a hope grounded in confidence in the Word of God. In today's fast-paced world of business, where everything changes so quickly, you need to draw strength from Abraham's story when hope appears to be gone. Since unrelenting courage comes from faith, you must keep faith alive when it seems impossible.

Obstacles and opposition (some of it spiritual in nature) surround every person's dream. It takes someone who won't give up to possess his or her dream. You must contend with the opposition and stand your ground until you see your dream come true. Declare, by faith, your position. Say: "I choose the top, and I am getting there. I have chosen victory. I must have it! Nothing will stop me. I must get there!" Faith and courage don't work unless you declare it. When you believe it, you will say it. If you can't say it, you don't believe it, and you won't fight for it. What you have not said, you have not believed and what you don't say, you will never see.

Business $mart Principle *The future that you don't declare, you don't deserve. Fight for your dream with unrelenting courage.*

8

The Winning Edge

Why Some Small Businesses Make a Killing and Others Fail

Here is a pop quiz. Ready?
Five frogs sit on a lily pad.
One decides to jump off.
How many are left? [1]

If your answer is *four,* your math skills are just fine. Unfortunately, this isn't a math problem. It's a life problem.

The correct answer is *five.* Yes, all five are still sitting on the lily pad. One frog only *decided* to jump. He hasn't actually done it yet.

So many of us have dreams we are not pursuing. We have great ideas to establish and grow a business, but we *sit on it,* waiting and waiting to jump off into the world of business but never making the leap.

❖ Book Smart versus Street Smart

Plenty of business owners invest a good amount of time and effort accumulating knowledge, but still end up with failed businesses. *Why?* Because mastering information only measures the *quantity* of your learning, not necessarily the *quality* of your learning.

❖ Winning Through Common Sense and Intuition

As I conduct business day-to-day, I'm often approached by people wanting to know the secret to success, i.e., the *magic formula*.

"What is the one thing I can do," they will say, "to guarantee my success?" My answer is to study the process, use common sense, and work your butt off.

Taking the *winning edge* in business is simply playing the game of business. One may ask, "What is the *game* of business?"

The *game* of business is the ability to put your competition away. I believe every successful business owner must possess the *killer instinct*. The mindset of a champion is that he or she is *never* ahead. This is a unique *winning edge* trait. Champions distort reality to serve their competitive purpose.

Champions have a *winning edge* ability to always come back from behind, even when the score indicates they are being destroyed by an opponent.

Champions must take everything they know about their competition and everything they allowed the competition to know about themselves and use that information to load the deck. This *Business Smart* principle will tilt your situation back to your advantage. This is called winning through common sense or intuition. Remember, sometimes you have to rely on your gut instinct. In this book, we have learned "gut instinct" is a component of *The God Factor,* which is not taught in business school.

❖ Know the Facts

You can't take the *winning edge* in the world of business until you have first looked at the facts. Facts alone won't guarantee you the *winning edge*, but they can protect you from handing it over to someone else. Unless you know all about your competition, you are dealing from a partial deck.

Let's assume the *one* fact you don't know—maybe because it's hard to find out—might be the *one* that will make the difference. Do not take any short cuts in this area. You must do the necessary hard work. Take the time and make the effort to learn everything you can about the company and the people you are working with. Learn the operative facts that define the company. This will set you apart and give you the *winning edge*.

I learned a lot in business from intuition. Imperative facts arise out of everyday situations. Pay attention to the things people *say* and *do*. These *winning edge cues* provide new and useful insights. I have seen, heard, and been involved in countless business situations where the emergence or the sensing of a single fact totally changed the dynamics or the tactics of everything that followed.

❖ Size up the situation

The whole point in gaining the *winning edge* in the marketplace is to know the facts. One way to read the market is to read people. Once you know the particulars and the players, and have analyzed all the ramifications, you can start to size up a situation. Take a step back and see what opportunities exist at the outset so you can gain the *winning edge*.

❖ Know Your Employees

As a business owner, constantly try to recognize real talent and not be misled by appearances. Hiring *quality* people, in lieu of a quantity of people, ensures your business maintains the *winning edge*.

Gaining the *winning edge* in the marketplace means you must hire some of the best people in your field of business. They will take your business to the top. Don't make the mistake of cutting corners when recruiting employees and building your team. I learned this principle the hard way.

❖ Thinking on Your Feet

In the world of business, you must learn to think on your feet to take the *winning edge*. As a general *Business Smart* principle, I am dedicated to the importance of *acting* instead of *reacting* and never *overreacting* in any business situation. The only exception to this may be a circumstance in which a *winning edge* or opportunity must be taken advantage of immediately before it disappears forever.

To reemphasize, the need to be opportunistic and to think on your feet underscores the importance of not only hearing, but acting on what people are saying. Your response to this knowledge positions you to take the *winning edge*.

Business Smart Principle

Don't make the mistake of dismissing what people are saying about your business.

❖ Focus Is Power in Business

Focus is simply a word. Because of its simplicity, it is often abused, not respected, and misunderstood. What most people miss is that focus is power. It will give you the *winning edge*. People who can focus are able to simultaneously gather all their abilities and direct their attention to the task or goal at hand. Focus is essential to take the *winning edge* in business. Successful businesses are made up of people who can focus.

As business owners, we must stay focused on our target. Even when the competition is trying their best to close you down, stay focused on your target. To take the *winning edge* is to eliminate distractions. Do not allow yourself to be distracted. To gain the *winning edge,* practice the power of focus.

To win the prize, you must focus. In a world where everything is moving at such a rapid pace, we must commit to live a life of focus if we are going to gain the *winning edge* in the marketplace. Jesus illustrated this principle in Matthew 7:7 when He told His disciples: "Ask, and it will be given to you; seek, and you will find; knock, and it will be opened to you." Jesus encouraged His disciples to press on and not lose sight of their goals.

Health, wealth, and happiness are reflections of a person's ability to focus their personal power to achieve what they want in life.

Business $mart Principle: *Gain the competitive edge by forming positive habits.*

Habit is Power in Business

There are two types of habits: those that serve you, and those that don't. Brushing your teeth every day is a habit that serves you. Not brushing your teeth is a habit that doesn't serve you. In order to succeed in the world of business, one must create and infuse great business habits into their life that command the *winning edge*.

Business owners reach the top by applying *Business Smart* principles, which include an appreciation for creating and practicing *winning edge* strategies. Determining to use these strategies creates *Business Smart* habits.

Be quick to break the habits that are breaking your business and hasten to adopt proven, *winning edge* strategies. As you adopt and regularly implement *winning edge* strategies, *Business Smart* habits are formed to achieve the results you desire—a successful, sustainable, growing, and profitable business.

9

Staying in Business

Everyone who starts a business wants to stay in business long enough to become successful. Starting a business doesn't automatically guarantee success, or else everyone who started a business would be successful.

Most young business owners want their businesses to grow at a rapid pace. If they are not growing fast, they think they are failing.

Why Do Some Small Businesses Fail?

Business failure isn't something you want to think about when you start a business. But, if you want to stay in business long enough to succeed, you need to know the things to *do* that will keep you in business. There are also things to *avoid* that will keep your business from being successful.

In this chapter, I share additional *Business Smart* principles to show you the things to *do* and things to *avoid*, which will empower you to operate your business long enough to succeed.

How to Stay in Business:

1. Avoid starting a business for the wrong reasons.

I have learned that starting a business simply because you want to make lots of money, be your own boss, and have more time with your family are not enough to produce a successful business. While these are surely benefits some successful entrepreneurs achieve after years of hard work, they are not reasons to start a business.

The right reasons I believe for starting a business that will lead to success are:

- Have a passion and love for what you will be doing. It will get you out of bed every day with the necessary drive to go out and face the *giants*.
- Believe your product and service will fulfill a real need in the marketplace.
- Have a relentless drive, determination, patience, and a positive attitude.
- When others fail and the *going gets tough*, you become more determined than ever to carry out the second half of the expression: *the tough get going*.
- Failure doesn't stop you. I have learned over the years that failure is a part of the process. You learn from your mistakes and use those lessons as business tips to help you succeed the next time around. I learned this lesson from many successful business owners. They all have attributed much of their success to building on earlier failures.

Business $mart Principle

Change your perception of failure. Perceive failure as a crucial step in the learning process.

2. There must be a need for what you are doing.

The best business ideas will fail if there isn't a market for what you are selling, or if the market suddenly disappears because of a change in the economy or a natural disaster.

Before you start a business, determine if there's a market for what you plan to sell *and* if that market is big enough for your business to be profitable.

Pay attention to this principle that *Business Smart* owners *must* understand: *everyone isn't a market*. Your market must be an identifiable group of customers you will be able to reach with the marketing dollars and resources you invest.

To avoid business failure after startup, business owners need to keep tabs on their market and their customers' changing needs.

3. Eliminate poor management.

Many a report on business failures cites poor management as the number one reason for failure. New business owners frequently lack relevant business and management expertise in areas such as finance, purchasing, selling, production, and hiring and managing employees. [1]

As a *Business Smart* owner, you must recognize what you don't do well and seek help. Otherwise, the company may fail and go out of business.

A successful manager is a good leader who creates a work climate that encourages productivity. They are skilled at hiring competent people and training them, and can delegate responsibilities. Good leaders are skilled strategic thinkers. They can turn a vision into a reality and confront change.

4. Insufficient capital is a common business mistake that leads to failure.

To stay in business long enough to see success, you must have sufficient operating funds. New business owners often don't understand cash flow or underestimate how much money they will need to get the business started. As a result, they are forced to close before they had a fair chance to succeed. They also may have an unrealistic expectation of incoming revenues from sales.

It is imperative to ascertain how much money your business will require. You must know not only how much it will cost to start your business, but the cost of staying in business. Most businesses take a year or two to get going. This means you will need enough funds to cover all the costs until sales can eventually pay for those costs.

5. Avoid over-expansion.

A leading cause of business failure is over-expansion. This often happens when business owners confuse success with how fast they can expand their business. It is hard for a new business owner to focus on slow, steady growth to achieve success. The mistake is to force growth by expansion, which often leads to failure.

At the same time, you do not want to repress growth. Once you have established a solid customer base and a good cash flow, let your success help you set the right measured pace. Look for indicators that signal the need for expansion, such as your current ability to keep up with production demands. Outgrow your present space. With careful study, review, research, and analysis, identify *what* and *who* you need to add for your business to grow. Then with the right systems and people in place, you can focus on the growth of your business.

Business Smart *Principle*
Do not try to do everything yourself.

Stay in business long enough to see success by using these *Business Smart* principles:

- ✓ Stay organized
- ✓ Be willing to make sacrifices
- ✓ Keep detailed records
- ✓ Know your competition
- ✓ Be creative
- ✓ Provide the best customer service
- ✓ Produce the best product

10

Surround Yourself with Human Inspiration

Inspiration is a key factor in any entrepreneur's quest for success. If you have no one inspiring you on your journey through life, then you will probably not go too far. Sir Isaac Newton is the English scientist and mathematician most famously known for his discovery of the law of gravity. He made numerous other discoveries, such as the law of inertia and the sun's place at the center of the planetary system. Indeed, he recorded so many that future generations of scientists coined the term "Newtonian" to describe bodies of knowledge that owed their existence to his theories. This brilliant man—who actually wrote more about theology than science—once said, "If I have seen further than others, it is by standing upon the shoulders of giants."[1] *Merriam-Webster's Dictionary* gives the following definition of *inspiration:*

> Inspiration: a divine influence or action on a person believed to qualify him or her to receive and communicate sacred revelation; the action or power of moving the intellect or emotions; the act of influencing or suggesting opinions . . . the quality or state of being inspired; an inspiring agent or influence.[2]

In other words, inspiration is a thing or person with powerful influence. This is why the Bible encourages us to surround ourselves with human inspiration. As the writer of Hebrews said:

> And we desire that each one of you show the same diligence to the full assurance of hope until the end, that you do not become sluggish, but imitate those who through faith and patience inherit the promises.
> - Hebrews 6:11–12

This Scripture shows how you can draw inspiration from someone who has achieved success in a pursuit similar to the one in which you are interested. Wise people will surround themselves with those who are wise: "He who walks with wise men will be wise, but the companion of fools will be destroyed" (Proverbs 13:20).

Business $mart Principle *In order to achieve greatness, you must surround yourself with human inspiration.*

Every human will reference himself as a product of others. No one has ever become a reference without having a reference for himself or herself. Every great person is connected to another great person. No one is an island unto themselves. To achieve greatness, surround yourself with others who have already achieved or can encourage you on the road to achievement. They will help you realize (and manifest) your dream. Rub shoulders with those who have accomplished great things while avoiding complainers, gripers, and whiners. You know the type. I call them the "woulda, coulda, shoulda" crowd.

❖ I *would* have done something great if only . . .
❖ I *could* have done something great if only . . .
❖ I *should* have done something great but . . .

As the old saying goes, *you can never spend excuses.*

Drawing Strength from Others

Solomon was full of wisdom and understanding. People came from all over the earth to hear his wisdom, from which they drew great inspiration:

> And God gave Solomon wisdom and exceedingly great understanding, and largeness of heart like the sand on the seashore. Thus Solomon's wisdom excelled the wisdom of all the men of the East and all the wisdom of Egypt. For he was wiser than all men—than Ethan the Ezrahite, and Heman, Chalcol, and Darda, the sons of Mahol; and his fame was in all the surrounding nations. He spoke three thousand proverbs, and his songs were one thousand and five. Also he spoke of trees, from the cedar tree of Lebanon even to the hyssop that springs out of the wall; he spoke also of animals, of birds, of creeping things, and of fish. And men of all nations, from all the kings of the earth who had heard of his wisdom, came to hear the wisdom of Solomon.
> - 1 Kings 4:29–34

Thousands of years after this wise king lived, we still need to surround ourselves with human inspiration to make business work. We draw strength from others. God gives every human being the spirit of inspiration, as affirmed by

Job: "But there is a spirit in man, and the breath of the Almighty gives him understanding" (Job 32:8). Human beings who draw inspiration from others, and couple it with divine understanding that only God can give—another component of *The God Factor*, make an unbeatable combination for success in their *Business Smart* endeavor.

When we inspire others through mutual sharing and understanding, we can walk alongside each other and see dreams come true that are bigger than any one person's ability to achieve. Leaders are a key, but so are those who follow them. We need each other. I like the way authors Dan Sullivan and Catherine Nomura bring this out in their book, *The Laws of Lifetime Growth*:

> Only a small percentage of people are continually successful over the long run. These outstanding few recognize that every success comes through the assistance of many other people and they are continually grateful for this support. Conversely, many people whose success stops at some point are in that position because they have cut themselves off from everyone who has helped them. They view themselves as the sole source of their achievements. As they became more self-centered and isolated, they lost their creativity and ability to succeed. Continually acknowledge others' contributions and you will automatically create room in your mind and in the world for much greater success. You will be motivated to achieve even more for those who have helped you. Focus on appreciating and thanking

others, and the conditions will always grow to support your increasing success.³

Never forget that if you want to be successful, you will need the support of many people. If you are wise, you will appreciate and acknowledge their contributions to your success. An entrepreneurial visionary without someone to inspire him or her will not go too far in their business journey. As the English poet and clergyman John Donne said in his famous poem: "No man is an island, entire of itself, every man is a piece of the continent, a part of the main."⁴

Inspiration Improves Business Performance

When you have a human reference from which you draw inspiration, you will be energized and empowered to complete your vision or project. Dean Tjosvold, a management professor at Simon Fraser University in British Columbia, has done considerable studies on the differences in behavior between people working cooperatively in groups and those who work competitively.

In the cooperation model, people realize they are successful when others succeed. Thus, they are oriented to help each other to perform effectively. They encourage each other because they understand that helping the other person meet his or her priorities will also help them. Compatible goals promote trust; people expect help and assistance from others and are confident they can rely on them. Expecting to get and give assistance helps them disclose their intentions and feelings. Therefore, they more freely offer ideas and resources and request aid. They are able to work out arrangements of exchange that leave all better off. These interactions result in friendliness, cohesion, and high morale.

Competitors, by contrast, feel threatened by others' success since it may frustrate their self-centered aspirations. They only come closer to their goals when others perform ineffectively. Competitors suspect that others will not help them. For to do so would only harm their own chances. Indeed, they may be tempted to try to mislead and interfere in order to better their performance. They are reluctant to discuss their needs and feelings, to ask others for help, or offer assistance. Closed off to drawing influence from others for fear of being exploited, they see their only methods of affecting others as coercion or threats. Therefore, their interactions result in frustration, hostility, and low productivity, especially in joint tasks.

Workers in China are often better able to forge cooperative relationships because of the Chinese cultural value of "saving face," Tjosvold said after a research project there. The professor called it important because it confirms an individual's desire to maintain such strong relationships. This enables stronger teamwork because instead of avoiding conflict people forge ahead to resolve issues:

> Showing respect for each other's face means that individuals are able to discuss their different perspectives and integrate their ideas constructively because they believe they are working together for mutual goals . . .
>
> Conflicts are more constructive when people try to resolve them for mutual benefit; conflicts involving

goal incompatibility and ethical issues can be more difficult. Rather than suppress ethical issues, if they can be discussed open-mindedly and codes of conduct used as guides, the issues can be dealt with constructively.[5]

The bottom line is that people who foster collaboration among themselves are much more likely to be more successful than those who promote competition. If you don't have anyone in your life from whom you can draw inspiration to help you in this fast-paced world of business, it won't be long before you give up.

Keys to Finding Inspiration

Here are seven keys to surrounding yourself with human inspiration:

1. Admit Your Weakness

No one knows it all or possesses every trait needed for success in business. Every man and woman has strengths and weaknesses. One can't minimize their weaknesses if they fail to admit they exist. Once we admit to ourselves we are weak in a particular area, we will seek out those around us with expertise. Namely, people who are growing and have more potential in the area in which they specialize. Before selecting people to associate with, ask yourself: *Is their attitude an asset or a liability? Do they love what they do and are they doing well?*

Business Smart Principle — *When you surround yourself with quality people, you will be inspired to share your weaknesses, learn, and grow.*

2. Develop Security in Yourself

Accepting yourself as you are, flaws included, is a hallmark of maturity. Famed medical researcher and virologist Jonas Salk, who developed the Salk polio vaccine, had many critics despite his incredible contribution to medicine. Introduced in 1957, his vaccine stemmed one of the most devastating epidemics in American history. Five years earlier, nearly 58,000 cases of polio were reported, with more than 3,100 deaths and 21,000 people left with mild or disabling paralysis. Salk observed that critics will first tell you that you're wrong, and then they will tell you that you're right—but what you're doing really isn't important. Finally, they will admit that you are right and that what you're doing is important; but, after all, they knew it all along!

How do leaders who are *out front* handle this kind of fickle response from others? They learn to accept themselves. After all, if you have endeavored to know yourself and worked hard to change yourself, what more can you do? Professor and best-selling author Leo Buscaglia says, "The easiest thing to be in the world is you. The most difficult thing to be is what other people want you to be. Don't let them put you in that position."[6]

"To be the best person you can be, and the best leader, you need to be yourself," says leadership expert John Maxwell. "That doesn't mean that you are not willing to grow and change, it just means that you work to become the best you can be. As psychologist Carl Rogers remarked: 'The curious paradox is that when I accept myself just as I am, then I change. Being who you really are is the first step in becoming better than you are. You will not surround yourself with human inspiration if you are not secure with yourself.'"[7]

3. Learn to Handle Criticism

Not everyone is going to agree with you. As an entrepreneur working to manifest your business dream, you will automatically face criticism. So, what should you do to avoid becoming a solo leader who tries to *go at it alone*? Take a realistic view of yourself, which will lay the foundation for successfully handling criticism. Learn to separate yourself from whatever prompts negative remarks. Is it about what you are doing—namely the project and your leadership position? Or is it about you, the person? You need to be able to separate the two, which you can only do when you know yourself. Learn not to take criticism personally when it isn't directed at you.

Maxwell's book, *Leadership Gold*, provides three ways to deal with criticism:

- Who criticized me? Adverse criticism from a wise person is more to be desired then enthusiastic approval of a fool. The source often matters.
- How was the criticism given? I try to discern whether the person was being judgmental or whether he gave me the benefit of the doubt and spoke with kindness.

- Why was it given? Was it given out of personal hurt or for my benefit? Remember, hurt people hurt people; they lash out or criticize to try to make themselves feel better, not to help the other person.[8]

4. Swallow Your Pride

Earlier, I mentioned how people came from miles around to learn from Solomon's wisdom. Listen to his words on the subject of pride: "Pride goes before destruction, and a haughty spirit before a fall. Better to be of a humble spirit with the lowly, than to divide the spoil with the proud" (Proverbs 16:18–19). Pride demonstrates an attitude of independence—from God and man. Pride will not allow you to feel the need to seek advice. Pride deceives you by making you feel as though the world is out to get you.

When people are consumed by pride, they will find themselves thinking they have all the answers and don't need anyone else. They ask, "Why should I seek human guidance?" The Bible is clear about pride: it is not part of God's plan for our lives. Another Proverb says, "A man's pride will bring him low, but the humble in spirit will retain honor" (Proverbs 29:23). The Psalmist wrote, "Though the LORD is great, he cares for the humble, but he keeps his distance from the proud" (Psalm 138:6 NLT). To escape from pride, we must humble ourselves before God and recognize we need both His wisdom and human guidance to succeed. Put away pride and seek the company of the wise.

5. Embrace Those Ahead of You

There are men and women who have accomplished great things in life. We can learn from those who have mastered their field. Because I adopt the attitude that I am a learner, I am constantly learning on a daily basis. I have great appreciation for those who have already reached where I want to go. Although, I can't meet with many of them personally, I can read their books, glean from their wisdom, and become a better person. The legendary Greek philosopher, Plato, once said, "The greater part of instruction is being reminded of things you already know."[9] As a pastor and businessman, I try to learn how others have done it. By following this pattern, I gain new insights and clearer understanding of situations. I seek to practice the wisdom of Solomon: "Walk with the wise and become wise; associate with fools and get in trouble" (Proverbs 13:20 NLT). Today I stand on the shoulders of many great men and women, who have added value to my life.

Business Smart Principle *A wise person learns from others' mistakes.*

6. Learn to Listen

If you are doing all the talking, you will soon find yourself alone. As Maxwell says:

> Understanding people precedes leading them; leadership finds its source in understanding. To be worthy of the responsibility of leadership, a person must have insights into the human heart. Sensitivity

toward the home and dreams of people on your team is essential for connecting with them and motivating them.[10]

In his bestselling book, *The 21 Irrefutable Laws of Leadership*, Maxwell shares that leaders must touch a heart before they ask for a hand. In other words, you cannot connect with someone if you don't try to first listen to and understand them. It is not fair to ask for help from someone when you haven't listened to his or her heart. You can't learn if you don't listen. Listening will increase your overall accomplishments.

7. Recognize Your Need for Mentors and Supporters

I surround myself with both. Mentors have taught me and guided me, even though I haven't met most of them. They have taught me through their books. These mentors reach across time and space to instruct me as I read about their research, ideas, and experiences. I also pull from what others have written about them. Their legacy lives on in me today.

There are others I have personally sought out since the early days of my pastoral and business endeavors. For example, I have traveled to Chicago to sit under the teaching of Dr. Robb Thompson. Dr. Thompson has taught me the principles of excellence in ministry. Atlanta Pastor Dr. Creflo Dollar has taught me how to develop my faith to believe for the impossible. My spiritual father is Dr. David Oyedepo, presiding bishop of Living Faith Church Worldwide, with a network of churches across Nigeria and most of Africa. He is the senior pastor of Faith Tabernacle, an impressive place with a seating capacity of fifty thousand. He pioneered the Education Institution Covenant University and Landmark University, where he serves as chancellor. I have learned so much from this great man. I listen to his teachings daily; they have helped sharpen my thinking and improve my leadership ability. Most of the good things that have happened to me are a direct result of great mentors. They are the people who reach down to draw me up to their level.

Supporters are those people who know me and offer their assistance intentionally. My supporters lift me up and make me better than I could be on my own. They are the "go to" people I seek when I need encouragement. Likewise, surround yourself with people who will inspire you. Learn from them and you will be better equipped to *Make Business Work for You.*

11

For Entrepreneurs Only

Entrepreneurs are Different

> One of the most dramatic cultural shifts over the last thirty years has been a redefinition of the *Great American Dream*. People are no longer content to work for two cars and a house in the right school district. Today the enjoyment of the job itself may be even more important than the enjoyment of its tangible rewards.
>
> - Errol Beckford

How many of you are tired of being employees, working 9-to-5, struggling financially, being dependent on others, and being unable to afford your credit card bills? Or are you the one not willing to follow where the path *may* lead you and are eager to create your own path? I bet the majority of people reading this book can relate. Although having given lots of thought to the idea of achieving your dream and being financially independent, like many, you may still be hesitant or simply not know where to start.

There is a special breed of people who are convinced they will never achieve total job satisfaction by working for someone else. I am one of those people. This is why I titled this chapter, "For Entrepreneurs Only."

Well, let's start by really understanding the term *entrepreneur*, as defined by dictionary.com:

> Entrepreneur: a person who starts, organizes and manages any enterprise, especially a business, usually with considerable initiative and risk.

Rather than working as an employee, an entrepreneur runs a small business and assumes all the risks and rewards of a given business venture, idea, or goods or services offered for sale.

You have in your hands more than *just* another business book or a self-help book. You have the beat of my heart. I am a follower of Jesus and have never been interested in maintaining the status quo. I am a pastor and passionate about serving God and answering the questions our business community is asking. I have learned that maintaining the status quo serves neither God nor the people He loves.

I am sold out to the vision and practices of the *entrepreneurial spirit*. I never want to be limited by what already exists. Instead, I aspire to pursue what should be. This is why I have dedicated this chapter to entrepreneurs only.

You will learn what makes *Business Smart* entrepreneurs different. This chapter is for people who are already entrepreneurs and also those who would like to be. This is not a chapter written by a college professor who *only* teaches entrepreneurship. It doesn't paint a rosy picture or provide a clinical step-by-step path to success. Both are unrealistic, and this book is very realistic. That's because it is written by an entrepreneur who has won, failed, and battled back to win again and again.

The entrepreneur's ability to dream, win, lose, and win again and again is what I call the *entrepreneurial spirit*. It is what separates the entrepreneur from everyone else in business. It is also what separates those who want to be entrepreneurs from those who *can* be entrepreneurs.

This is a crucial point to understand. The entrepreneurial spirit is not about numbers, not about growth plans, and not about increasing revenue. Nor is it about increasing production and expanding the company.

The entrepreneurial spirit is all about confronting challenges and obstacles, while believing God and *The God Factor* He has given you to possess success is bigger than anything that tries to oppose your dream. It demands courage to develop and implement bold strategies to accomplish new vision. We must remember no government can create real jobs. Only entrepreneurs can do that. Only entrepreneurs can see the future and bring it to life through the progression of risk, loss, and winning over and over. In the process, they create new industries and opportunities for people all over the world.

Another problem is that schools do not create entrepreneurs. Schools are designed to create employees. This is why people say, "Go to school to get a good job." Most students, even graduates of MBA programs, go on to become employees, not entrepreneurs.

How Do You Know if You Possess the Entrepreneurial Spirit?

Here are five characteristics every entrepreneur *must* have:
1. They understand the creative process.
2. They are always ready to learn and execute their learning.
3. They are proactive.
4. They take risks and make mistakes.
5. They have removed self-limiting boundaries.

Qualities of Successful Entrepreneurs

As a *Business Smart* entrepreneur, I will share ten qualities that make a successful entrepreneur:

1. **Vision**
   A *Business Smart* entrepreneur is able to create and deliver a clear mission statement outlining the purpose and function of a new venture in order to launch the business successfully. They are an electrifying inspiration to others and can recruit people to join their enterprise.

2. **Self-driven and Passionate**
   Business Smart entrepreneurs are self-driven by the passion they possess for the project they are pushing. Without passion, a business owner will quit as soon as they hit the first roadblock. Believing in what you are doing helps overcome critics and skeptics. Be driven by your belief that the idea is going to work. Passion is a crucial ingredient to win support and achieve success.

3. **Self-starter**

    Business Smart entrepreneurs are self-starters. They motivate themselves daily to do better each day than the previous day. Striving for excellence begets advancement and growth. Renowned internet marketer Neil Patel says, "Motivation is like jet power propulsion. It transforms individuals from passive participants into active leaders."[1]

    Business Smart entrepreneurs know what they are meant to do in life. They don't need to be told what they should do daily. They prepare themselves mentally for each day and their motivation never runs low.

4. **Innovative**

    All *Business Smart* entrepreneurs are highly innovative. They provide innovative solutions to existing or foreseen problems. They are good at nurturing ideas.

    Business Smart entrepreneurs will take an idea and incessantly think about the idea and try to find out ways to make it work. If you ask them about the idea later, chances are they will have a plan to turn that idea into reality.

5. **Determined**

    Business Smart entrepreneurs are aware they will face obstacles and people will question their ideas and their credibility. They factor that into their journey and appreciate not everyone will believe in their ideas and vision. *Business Smart* entrepreneurs believe *it* before they see *it*.

6. **Courageous**

   Business Smart entrepreneurs are not afraid of failing and being criticized. They are aware they could lose everything following their dream if they fail. Nevertheless, they have the courage to pursue their goals again and again until they succeed.

7. **Creativity**

   Business Smart entrepreneurs inject imagination and uniqueness into their business. Creativity is an essential skill required to bring forth a model and right strategies to develop readiness in all aspects to beat the competition.

8. **Self-discipline**

   Self-discipline appears in different forms, such as perseverance, restraint, endurance, thinking before acting, finishing what you start, and the ability to carry out decisions and plans, despite inconveniences or obstacles. Being self-controlled and having the ability to avoid unhealthy excess of anything that could lead to negative consequences helps you to successfully pursue your business goals.

9. **Know How to Pivot**

   Business Smart entrepreneurs adapt. Not because somebody tells them to, but because of an adjustment they need to make to a product or service, or to better meet customers' needs.

While *Business Smart* entrepreneurs are passionate about their idea, they know the ultimate goal is to make the world better by helping customers. If they realize their idea needs a pivot, even a painful one, they will follow through.

10. Confident and Humble

Business Smart entrepreneurs are certain their idea is important, but recognize it is usually a long path to success. They show the right balance of confidence and humility. They know different people have different levels of understanding regarding components of projects and *Business Smart* entrepreneurs adapt. Not being humble or being too confident alienates potential help.

Business Smart entrepreneurs consciously practice these traits. If you desire to start a business or already have one, honestly analyze *if* you consistently practice these traits. It is not enough to just read about or know them. They must be fully implemented.

If you don't have these traits nor a desire to develop these traits, you should not start a business. It will lead to frustration and disappointment. My advice to you is: *you are better off working for someone else*. This does not eliminate you from being a future *Business Smart* entrepreneur. Glean from your employer and the marketplace. Research and develop your idea. In the future, you may embark on the journey of entrepreneurship. Review chapter 2 to reiterate the importance of *timing*.

On the other hand, if you possess these traits, and have not yet stepped out on faith to do *it*, my advice to you is: *Get started! What are you waiting for?*

In a world of high unemployment with an economy that needs new jobs to recover, who isn't hungry for a solution—for something that brings about recovery fast? Today many of us look to the government for answers, but it's becoming obvious that governments can't create real jobs.

The truth is, only one group of people can bring our world back to prosperity. Entrepreneurs are that group of people, and particularly entrepreneurs who are *Business Smart*.

Business Smart entrepreneurs create the most jobs and the most prosperity for the most people. They are the ones who win.

If you are struggling with your business: *Don't Give Up On Your Dream*. Stay until you win. Ask God for help. Incorporate *The God Factor*, overcome *Fear of Failure*, and apply the given *Business Smart* planning principles to your endeavor.

About the Author

Errol Beckford is the founding and senior pastor of Celebration Tabernacle Church in Cocoa, Florida. He is the author of Make Life Work and host of the daily radio program, *Make Your Day Count.*

Errol Beckford is a gifted teacher, business developer, business coach, and a graduate of New York's prestigious school of business, New York University.

His marketplace approach to ministry is one of his most notable accomplishments. Under the leadership of Errol Beckford, Celebration Tabernacle Church, Inc. acquired and developed two local commercial plazas, both within half a mile of the church.

This book, *Business Smart*, is comprised of over twenty-six years of life development skills. Errol Beckford's passion is to help people succeed in life. The most rewarding part of his life's work is helping people overcome failure and achieve success.

An advocate for empowering people to take control of their lives, he is dedicated to share what he has learned over the years to those thinking of starting their own business and those who already have a business and want it to grow.

Before you waste any more time and money, you owe it to yourself, your family, and the world to discover and master the principles of *Business Smart.*

There are thousands of business books. This book is for young entrepreneurs. It teaches you what business books and business schools won't. Use the *God Factor*, overcome *Fear of Failure.* and apply *Business Smart* principles to succeed in your business enterprises.

Please subscribe to Errol Beckford's YouTube channel:

Business Smart with Beckford

https://www.youtube.com/channel/UCuI1ftNwvxWf1QRbvFTrQ-A

Endnotes

Chapter 1: You Must Have a Business Plan
1. Julianne Koepcke, "How I Survived a Plane Crash," March 24, 2012, *BBC Magazine*, http://www.bbc.com/news/magazine-17476615.
2. Edmund Burke, September 21, 2021, *Forbes,* https://www.forbes.com/quotes/2430/.

Chapter 2: Intangibles of Building a Business
1. Victor Kiam, September 21, 2021, *Power Quotations,* https://powerquotations.com /quote/entrepreneurs-are-simply-those-who.

Chapter 4: Understanding the Market
1. Mark H. McCormack, *What They DON'T Teach You at Harvard Business School*, (Bantam, June 1, 1986), 70.

Chapter 5: Play by the Rules
1. Margaret Heffernan "How Warren Buffett defines integrity," MoneyWatch, Nov. 13, 2013, http://www.cbsnews.com/news/how-warren-buffett-defines-integrity/.
2. "What Warren Buffett Wants to Know Before He Hires You," Recruiter Box, http://recruiterbox.com/blog/what-warren-buffett-wants-to-know-before-he-hires-you/.
3. Stephanie Yang, "5 Years Ago Bernie Madoff Was Sentenced to 150 Years in Prison – Here's How His Scheme Worked," Prison-Here's how His Scheme.
4. "Billy Graham on the Need for Integrity," Billy Graham Library, June 25, 2014, http://lettersfromthelibrary.com/billy-graham-on-the-need-for-integrity/.
5. "Disgraced pastor Haggard admits second relationship with man," CNN, Jan. 30, 2009, http://www.cnn.com/2009/US/01/29/lkl.ted.haggard/Index.html.
6. Carlos Wallace, "Life is Not Complicated…" Sept. 30, 2014, https://authorcarloswallace.wordpress.com/2014/09/30/life-is-not-complicated-derek-jeter-a-man-of-integrity-discipline-and-consummate-professionalism/.
7. "Mariano Rivera Rescues, Renovates 107-Year-Old Church in New Rochelle," CBS New York, Mar. 6, 2014, http://newyork.cbslocal.com/2014/03/06/Mariano-rivera-rescues-renovates-church-in-new-rochelle/.

Chapter 7: The Power of Unrelenting Courage
1. "Noah Galloway Bio: About Noah," http://noahgalloway.com/about-noah/.
2. Lorin Wolfe, *The Bible on Leadership: From Moses to Matthew – Management Lessons for Contemporary Leaders*, (New York: AMACOM, 2002), 164.
3. Mary Kay, "Company and Founder: One of a Kind Success Story," http://www.marykay.com/en-us/about-mary-kay/companyfounder.

4. Bio, "Mary Kay Ash," http://www.biography.com/people/mary-kay-ash-197044.
5. Mary Kay, "Company Quick Facts," http://www.marykay.com/en-US/about-mary-kay/companyfounder/pages/company-quick-facts.aspx.
6. "Fred Smith: An Overnight Success," *Entrepreneur,* Oct. 28, 2008, http://www.entrepreneur.com/article/197542.
7. Ibid.
8. Keith Johnson, *The Confidence Makeover: The New and Easy Way to Quickly Change Your Life,* (Shippenburg, PA: Destiny Image Publishers, 2005), 238.

Chapter 8: The Winning Edge
1. Jeff Olson, *The Slight Edge*, (Greenleaf Book Group Press, 2013), 178.

Chapter 9: Staying in Business
1. Tom Rath / Barry Conchie, *Strengths Based Leadership,* (Gallup Press, 2008), 57.

Chapter 10: Surround Yourself with Human Inspiration
1. Brainy Quote®, "Isaac Newton quotes," http://www.brainyquote.com/quotes/quotes/i/isaacnewto135885.html.
2. Merriam-Webster Dictionary, definition of "inspiration," http://www.Merriam-webster.com/dictionary/inspiration.
3. Dan Sullivan and Catherine Nomura, *The Laws of Lifetime Growth,* (Oakland, CA: Berrett-Koehler Publishers, 2007), 43.
4. John Donne, "No Man Is An Island," http://www.poemhunter.com/poem/ode-19/#content.
5. "Cooperate conflict 'strengthens decision-making,'" November 2004 *Research Frontiers*, newsletter of the Research Grants Council of Hong Kong, China, http://www.ugc.edu.hk/rgc/rgcnews9/Pages/4b%20Conflicts-E.html.
6. GoodReads, "Leon Buscaglia Quotes," http://www.goodrads.com/Quotes/8739-the-easiest-thing-to-be-in-the-world-is-you.
7. John Maxwell, *Leadership Gold,* (Nashville, TN: Thomas Nelson Publishers, 2008), 37.
8. Ibid., 36.
9. Ibid., 37.
10. Ibid., 51.

Chapter 11: For Entrepreneurs Only
1. Neil Patel, "Entrepreneur," Retrieved Sept. 21, 2021, https://www.entrepreneur.com/article/305337

www.ingramcontent.com/pod-product-compliance
Lightning Source LLC
Chambersburg PA
CBHW071420070526
44578CB00003B/623